CONFLICT *OR* CONNECTION

Interpersonal Relationships in Cross-cultural Settings

LEVI KEIDEL

Published by Evangelical Missions Information Service
25W560 Geneva Rd.
Carol Stream, Ill. 60188
Box 794, Wheaton, Ill. 60189
(708) 653-2158
Printed in the United States of America

The Evangelical Missions Information Service (EMIS) publishes Evangelical Missions Quarterly and Pulse newsletter. The purpose of EMIS is to inform, motivate, and equip missionaries and to help shape the theories, values, and practices of the evangelical missionary enterprise.

Other EMIS publications: *Overcoming Missionary Stress* by Dr. Marjory Foyle ($9.95); *Don't Pig Out on Junk Food: An MKs Guide to Survival in the U.S.* by Alma Daugherty Gordon ($9.95).

For further information, write: EMIS, PO Box 794, Wheaton, Ill. 60189.

Keidel, Levi O.
    Conflict or connection: interpersonal relationships in cross-cultural settings / by Levi Keidel.
        p.   cm.
    Includes bibliographical references and index.
    ISBN 0-9617751-2-2 (alk. paper)
    1. Intercultural communication—Religious aspects—Christianity.
    2. Missions—Theory.   3. Christianity and culture.   4. Interpersonal relations—Religious aspects—Christianity.   I. Title.
    BV2082 .I57K45 1996
    266'.0023—dc20   96-21851
                                                          CIP

Contents

92438

Introduction

I n a previous book, I openly shared my personal struggles as a missionary (*Stop Treating Me Like God*, Carol Stream: Creation House, 1971). In it I tried to emulate the honest, vulnerable writing style Keith Miller made popular by his *Taste of New Wine* (Waco: Word, 1965) and *A Second Touch* (Waco: Word, 1967).

My book never made the best-seller lists. However, the response of missions-oriented people astonished me. The late J. Herbert Kane at Trinity International University, and others, used it as a text in their missions classes. Unsolicited affirmation came from people like Stuart Briscoe; Harvie Conn of Westminster Theological Seminary; and Philip Yancey, editor-at-large of *Christianity Today*. Missionaries in Kenya, Ecuador, Burundi, Zimbabwe, and the Philippines wrote of its impact upon their lives. Recently a Muslim mission agency spokesperson wrote, "Were it available, I would make it required reading for our candidates."

Now, in my retirement, I consider the possible value of a book which borrows a few ideas from my previous one, uses the same personalized style, but focuses specifically on the challenge of maintaining positive interpersonal relationships in a cross-cultural setting. On the one hand, my experiences are now dated; they derive from what missiologists term "a previous era." In the light of rapidly changing global realities, are such experiences relevant for the present?

On the other hand, principles for good interpersonal relationships are timeless. Factors such as urbanization, the growing chasm between rich and poor, heightening ethnic tensions and political instability, great blocks of gospel-resistant peoples, and the pluralizing trends in cultures, all make skills in cross-cultural relationships increasingly needful now, and more needful than at any time in the past. Hence, this effort, as was my previous one, is somewhat experimental. I hope it will similarly address unmet needs among persons committed to sharing the love of Christ effectively in a cross-cultural setting.

1

Eager Immaturity

By the time a missionary candidate finally arrives on the foreign field, enough has already happened to make him or her feel a bit extraordinary. I was no exception. For years I had read books, clipped news articles, and consulted missionaries, garnering every scrap of information that would help prepare me for ministering to the people of Zaire. A Bible school education gave me what were perceived as the best tools for that ministry. Speakers at missions conferences so inspired me that I felt ready, if necessary, to lay my head on the chopping block for Jesus.

Then came a rapid sequence of events which could not but color my feelings about myself and the future: my ordination and its serious vows of commitment; packing our belongings into barrels and preparing seemingly endless lists of their contents; trips to various hospitals to secure inoculations against strange diseases which would threaten us; the arrival of our passport with the stamped approvals of heads of governments; setting a departure date; and the farewell service, when Christian friends, with all the ebullience they could muster, reassured us of their faithful support during these pending years of separation.

My feelings were enhanced by a few additional credentials. During my late teenage years I'd been converted to Christ; this experience radically changed the direction of my life, and convinced me of the absolute authority of the message I was to preach. Moreover, my wife was at least as dedicated to Zaire as I was. The Lord had called Eudene to the mission field when she was nine; and when I began dat-

part harmony choral groups that sang with unprecedented zest and beauty. Students took great pleasure in their new found skills, enjoyed their prestige, and lauded their missionary teacher.

Meanwhile, Joe wanted to encourage and consolidate his village evangelists. He brought in marketable merchandise, and sold it to the evangelists at discount prices. He raised hogs. When evangelists came to the mission station for their quarterly salaries, he would kill and roast a hog for them. Profits from his commercial ventures subsidized the salaries of the evangelists. Their preferential treatment bonded them to their missionary supervisor.

The evangelism program grew, fostered by its economic advantages. David felt handicapped by his limited budget, and humiliated by this discrimination. Disagreement between the two missionaries came to separate them by a chasm. They stopped speaking to each other; they refused to attend services together.

Africans split into two parties, and served to inflame the dispute. I have an elderly Zairian friend who was a schoolboy then. He witnessed the final scenerio. In public the two men squared off and argued. They raised their voices in anger. African partisans watched with growing consternation. One missionary threw a colloquial insult; the other pulled out his belt and raised it to strike. They threatened blows, and were forcibly separated. Zairians, like Americans, tend to retell such stories with embellishments. The original version is lost in history, but its lesson was not lost on those who knew of the incident. After that time, attrition of personnel under our mission because of interpersonal conflicts was very low.

Back on our mission station, Ray and his wife would soon be leaving for a one-year furlough. Eudene and I would remain to carry on all missionary duties. One day a local layman, still young in the Christian faith, came to visit me. After the conventional pleasantries he said, "You know, we Africans have great joy that you are going to be our new leader. You have youth; you have strength; you have fresh ideas; you empathize with us. That older missionary was authoritarian; he wouldn't listen to us; he was so stuck in his ways. But now things are going to be different." We prayed about the new challenges that faced me, and he left.

Later that day I had occasion to visit Ray in his office. To confirm cordiality, I said, "Do you know what happened this morning?" I related the above incident to him. Ray chuckled, then said, "Do you want to know something else?"

"What?"

"The same fellow came to see me. He said the Africans were really concerned that I'm leaving. I'm experienced; I'm mature; I understand them. I've always run things hitherto. They just don't know what will happen, when all that responsibility falls into the hands of an inexperienced young buck like you!"

Our hearty laugh firmed a relational foundation stone: missionary unity. Only infrequently do relational issues provide an opportunity to laugh. Often, efforts to maintain positive working relationships over an extended period prove outright draining; and one does not always understand why.

3

A Grudge

We had been in the States on furlough for over a year. Our last term on the field had been unusually grueling. Any tired missionary fresh home on furlough suffers some stresses of psychological readjustment. But, ordinarily, a year is ample time for one to be refreshed, restored, and highly motivated to return.

But I wasn't. Depression and discouragement dogged me with pernicious mental and physical weariness. To this was added the stress of not knowing why. I certainly couldn't blame my circumstances. My doctor examined me and gave me a clean bill of health. I was not carrying heavy responsibility. I attended Bible lectures. I had ample time for study and meditation. My wife and children were happy. To my knowledge, everyone around me cared about me. But knowing that my circumstances were ideal didn't lift my spirits; rather, it depressed me further. It simply meant that the "why" of my problem would be more difficult to find.

A dentist and a few of his close friends offered to pay my way to a five-day laymen's institute on the West Coast. I was almost weary of seeing the familiar faces of others who were running the conference and convention circuits, and I was dubious that another conference would do anything remarkable for me. But this event proved different in more ways than one. I believe I found in it an important part of my answer. I was seated with several hundred laymen in the beautiful Mirror Room of palatial Arrowhead Springs Hotel in the foothills of the San Bernardino Moun-

tains of southern California. We had just finished breakfast, and were listening to Dr. Henry Brandt, a Christian
psychologist.

"Many men don't want to be happy," he said. "They'd
rather be mad than glad. They'd rather nurse a rankling
grudge. They cling to their misery and love it. I asked one
man why he was so bitter towards his wife. He said, 'I
want her to know how unhappy I am.'

"When a man harbors a grudge like that for 20 years, it
becomes as precious as an heirloom—a prized possession.
Every so often he takes it out, dusts it off, looks at it; he
couldn't do without it. To give it up is the supreme sacrifice."

Inwardly I agreed. I'd known people guarding festering
resentment like that.

"Such a man can't be a good man," Brandt continued.
"Whatever good he has is being drained from him by his
grudge. He is always depressed. His grudge structures his
total outlook on life. Ask a man like this, 'What was the
best thing that happened to you last week?' He'll say,
'What d'ya mean? I want to tell you what is wrong with
the world and why it's right for me to be mad at it.' His
bitterness spills out on everybody around him."

Then Brandt recounted an experience he'd had while
visiting Zaire. A veteran missionary came to him for counsel. This missionary was liked by the Zairians; he'd served
them faithfully. Disturbances connected with the coming of
political independence had so inflamed the atmosphere that
one of his most trusted church leaders had hotly offended
him and spit in his face.

Later, when the missionary returned, the church leader
apologized profusely. The missionary brushed it off as having been incidental. Then problems began to crop up in his
interpersonal relationships. They became so critical that
he seriously considered asking to be transferred to another
location.

After probing the man's past, Brandt helped him see
that while he had verbally forgiven his offender, deep down
his feelings of love and respect for the man had never been
fully restored. He'd been harboring a deeply buried grudge.

The bitterness of this grudge was now affecting relations with all who worked with him.

The solution was not a change of geographic location; the pattern would simply recycle itself. The only solution was recognizing the grudge as sin, confessing and renouncing it, refusing to give it further sanctuary, and committing himself, with the help of God, to love his brother fervently.

I had an uncanny sense of identification with that missionary. Maybe Brandt could help me. I knew the psychological surgery could be painful; but if there was some hidden abscess causing my trouble, this was the time to deal with it.

Brandt met me at the breakfast table the next morning. He wielded his scalpel with ruthless efficiency, located my problem, and laid it open for me to see. It was uglier than I wanted to admit.

On the field I had been given an important long-term assignment. I gave myself body and soul to discharging it. A gifted Zairian, Mr. A., was appointed to work with me. As time progressed, he became harassed with a growing number of complex domestic problems. He spent less and less time at work. He could not carry out his responsibilities. This seriously impaired the progress of our assignment.

During succeeding months tensions mounted. Frustration exhausted me. With the success of the project and my health at stake, I eventually insisted that the man be replaced. After a succession of long, draining palaver sessions, he was dismissed.

Some weeks later word reached me that a prominent church leader, Rev. B., had fixed me with blame for the entire incident.

"How do you feel toward Mr. A.?" Dr. Brandt asked me.

"I have no particular feelings about him. I don't hate him."

"But do you love him?"

"Well, when his domestic problems interrupted his work schedule, I took a lot of time trying to help him."

"Did you do it because you really loved him, or because

you wanted him to get back to work so the project would succeed?"

I was guilty.

"How do you feel about Rev. B?"

"I didn't gossip about his accusing me; I kept it to myself."

"Did you harbor ill feelings toward him?"

"Well, to be honest with you, I didn't feel the ill will I harbored toward him was as serious as his falsely accusing me. I simply kept my feelings to myself."

"He gossiped about you. Don't you see that you're patting yourself on the back for not gossiping about him? You're proud of the fact that you are better than he is. You're using that pride to salve your conscience against the grudge you are carrying. You're using your goodness to conceal your sin. Pull your grudges out into the open and expose them for the sin that they are.

"Hebrews 12:15 warns us that harboring a root of bitterness within you will trouble you; it will cause you to fail of the grace of God; it will defile those around you. Do you remember what Paul wrote in 1 Corinthians 13:5? 'Love does not keep a record of wrongs' (TEV). It's a good thing you didn't return to the field with these feelings; you'd surely have run into trouble."

Well, surgery was over. I needed space for recovery. I went outside and sat on the close-clipped lawn in the sunshine, and tried to further think through my problem. What is the source of a grudge? Resentment. Anger. What does a hidden grudge eventually spawn? A desire for revenge. Revenge is an ugly word. I didn't want to admit that it was one of my subdued desires. The patriarch Lamech manifested it in its most primitive form. He boasted to his wives, "I have slain a man for wounding me . . . If Cain is avenged sevenfold, truly Lamech (will be avenged) seventy-sevenfold" (Gen. 4:23, 24, RSV). Deep down, this is probably the kind of revenge we like most. It obliterates those who oppose us. It is the revenge of overkill.

But this kind of revenge endlessly recycled leads to annihilation. God couldn't watch this happen. So he introduced to Israel a new concept of revenge: "Thou shalt give life for life, eye for eye,. . . stripe for stripe" (Ex. 21:23-25). Man may not be happy with restricted revenge, but he can live with it. When Jesus came, he claimed to supersede the Mosaic concept of revenge. He said, "Love your enemies, bless them that curse you, do good to them that hate you, and pray for those who abuse use you" (Luke 6:27, 28, RSV). Human nature rejects this as totally unreasonable; or at best, impractical.

Take Peter, for example. He was human, and practical. He was ready to avenge with his sword the rights of his Lord. But by the time he was old, he'd come to see it Jesus' way: "If when you do right and suffer for it you take it patiently, you have God's approval. For to this you have been called, because Christ also suffered for you (wrongfully), leaving you an example, that you should follow in his steps. He committed no sin; no guile was found on his lips. When he was reviled, he did not revile in return; when he suffered, he did not threaten; but he trusted (himself) to him who judges justly. He himself bore our sins in his body on the tree, that we might die to sin and live to righteousness. By his wounds you have been healed" (1 Pet. 2:20-24, RSV).

Lamech said, "For wounding me, I killed." Jesus said, "For wounding me, I will heal." Inherent in vicarious suffering there seems to be a mystical power to heal. Jesus' power to heal arises from his having suffered vicariously for us.

The New Testament teaches that nothing warrants my holding any kind of grudge against anybody. It instructs me to leave vengeance in the hands of God, who by his very nature must judge justly. I am to reciprocate love to the one who has ill-treated me, and thereby release the power of my wounding for his healing. Jesus stated clearly that "if you do not forgive, neither will your Father who is in heaven forgive your trespasses," and he used the parable of the unforgiving servant to confirm it (Mk. 11:26; Mt. 18:23-35).

Of course, if I so choose, God allows me to enjoy my "delicious spites and darling angers," as Tennyson put it. But by doing so, I imply to God that I want to dispense judgment because I can do it more justly than he. This divorces me from God's grace. It effectively drains the situation of its healing, reconciling potential, and my concealed bitterness defiles, rather than heals, those around me.[1]

Sam Shoemaker put it another way. When we refuse to love and forgive our neighbor, the umbilical cord by which God feeds his forgiving and healing grace to us is severed; and into the vacuum rush fears and uncertainties about our own well-being.[2]

---

1. In those moments of waiting, God gave me grace to uproot and expose my grudges, and to confess them as sin. I gave my will to him to love people, in spite of who they are or what they might say about me. I left the conference feeling like a new man.

A harbored grudge is only one factor that damages interpersonal relationships. There is another factor, in cross-cultural settings, which often operates totally below our level of awareness. It's unrecognized racism (see Chapter 5).

2. Sam Shoemaker, *And Thy Neighbor*, ed. C. C. Offill (Waco: Word, 1967), p. 11.

4

Multicultural Teams

For most of the 20th century, the missionary team has been comprised of persons from a common culture living among a people of a different culture. Today the composition of the missionary team is changing. More and more, missionary teams are becoming multicultural.[1] Several factors account for this trend.

One is that the number of missionary candidates coming from Western countries is on the decline, while the number of candidates emerging from Asia, Africa, and Latin America is mushrooming. Also, technological advances in communications and transportation have shrunk our planet to a global village. For missions, the logical and inevitable consequence of these factors is a partnershiping of resources on an international level. This will require that missionary teams become multicultural.

In the previous two chapters we learned that missionaries must work hard to maintain harmonious interpersonal relationships if the team is to function effectively. The most common reason missionaries give for not returning to the field for a second term is interpersonal conflict within the missionary team. For the most part, persons on these teams come from a common culture.

Now, when persons from other cultures join the missionary team, interpersonal harmony becomes an even greater challenge. In the past, most first-term missionaries found that their primary problem was learning to communicate with the cross-cultural people they had come to serve. Now, candidates serving on multicultural teams are discovering that the greater problem of communication is between the team members themselves. Sandra Mackin, who has been working on multinational teams in the Philippines, describes some of these problems.[2]

> A Filipino missionary serving in Japan reports that her Dutch teammate is "against new ideas and insists on what she likes." Her German teammate is a "very negative lady who always complains and asks Why?" Her Australian teammate finds it difficult to accept Filipino leaders. A Pakistani missionary. . .was shocked by Filipino Christians having dates; he was hurt by his American director's busyness and failure to spend time with him. A Tonga missionary was hurt by his Indian leader's bluntness in correcting him. . .A Filipino pastor's wife, meaning to compliment me, told me I looked "sexy."

We Americans tend to assume that our culture is superior to other cultures. From this we deduce that our way of doing things is the "best" or the "only" way. Bringing such an attitude into a multicultural team can only portend trouble.

Cultures cannot be measured against each other as to quality. Each cultural grouping of people naturally feels that its culture is "the best." Strangeness of cultural behavior makes it neither good nor bad. What appears to us as "strange behavior" is, within the context of that culture, both appropriate and logical. Perhaps the most we can say is that each culture has its strengths and weaknesses, in informing humans how to behave.

Following are four areas which can be "mine fields" to harmony in a multicultural missionary team.[3] While "Americans" are generally understood as people from the U.S., in my view, the same basic attitudes apply for Canadians, but to a lesser degree.

1. Our Approach to Dialogue

Americans enter dialogue by asking each other superficial questions:

"How are you?"

"I am fine. How are you?"

"I am fine. How is your wife?"

No one expects a lengthy reply. But a question is necessary to trigger the next level of response. By reciprocating questions, the discussion eventually reaches a deeper level. When there is not another question, the dialogue stops.

Scandinavian people tend to be reflective. They readily dialogue about their inner feelings. The only questions needed are for further clarification. A Finn, for example, will share something of himself with a friend. He then expects the friend to share something of his own inner feelings.

So what happens when an American and a Finn meet?

The American asks, "How are you?" The Finn launches into a five-minute explanation of how he feels at the moment, and stops.

He expects the American to reciprocate, but is disappointed; the American needs a question to trigger a response. Inasmuch as no question is forthcoming from the Finn, the American terminates the embarrassing silence by asking another question. Again the Finn shares of himself, to a deeper level. The Finn waits for the American to reciprocate, but again he is disappointed. Because the Finn doesn't ask a question, the American asks another one to salvage the dialogue. In the end, both are disappointed. The Finn feels he has in effect been disrobed by the American's many questions, and the American has shared nothing of himself. The American feels the Finn has taken up all the time exposing his innermost feelings, but has denied the American opportunity to share his own feelings by failing to ask a question.

Our American disinclination to dialogue means that our relationships tend to be superficial. We are more comfortable advertising ourselves by distributing business cards, than we are engaging ourselves in deep dialogues. On the other hand, Europeans tend to cherish privacy. They slowly build lifetime relationships with a few carefully selected friends.

2. Our Choice of Words

We Americans select our words for impact. We overuse

superlatives: everything is wonderful, fantastic, tremendous, awesome. Characteristically, our superlatives are used to describe the positive rather than the negative aspects of a subject. Europeans feel that we have adopted the jargon of advertising; we exaggerate. For example, if I relate three events, describing each of them as "the most fantastic experience of my life," how can I be truthful? Consequently, when an American gives a report, Europeans will take her words at perhaps 60 percent of their value.

Europeans, on the other hand, select their words for accuracy. Rather than "always" and "never," they will say "often" and "seldom." In giving a report, Europeans will carefully describe the positive things, the negative things, and give reasons for the problems. We Americans will view such a report as overly pessimistic and lacking vision. It is "poor advertisement."

3. Forms of Logic Used in Problem Solving

Americans use linear logic in problem solving. I line up my points in order: 1, 2, 3, and 4; which cause me to arrive at point 5, a conclusion. Americans are inclined to gather the positive data which will help them reach their desired conclusion. The British also use linear logic, but bring into consideration the negative factors. They will choose the solution that can be reached with the least difficulty. In either case, the process is one-dimensional. Such logic works well in science and technology; but it would not work for a musician who wishes to compose a symphony.

When I arrived in Zaire to begin my missionary service, I soon discovered that my linear logic was out of place. Africans don't follow an outline. They solve problems contextually. By dialogue they paint the entire picture. They illustrate by proverbs or stories. If no solution is forthcoming, they dialogue further, painting the picture in finer detail. If they cannot reach consensus, they live with the problem. They would rather make no decision at all than make one that disrupts harmony, or is wrong.

Frequently, I was a member of a Zairian problem-solving committee. I would listen openly, then impatiently, then with mounting frustration, finally with virtual exasperation. "They are just going around in circles," I would tell myself. "When are they ever going to come to the point?" Once, when I chaired the committee, we were caught in what seemed to me an endless circling of dialogue. I proposed we bring the issue to a vote. "No!" the Zairians unanimously protested. "That would force us to take sides, and make enemies among us."

Europeans use forms of contextual logic. The form popular in Germany is dialectical. The German's characteristic response to a thesis is, "Yes, but. . ." after which he states the other side of the issue as antithesis. This polarizes the issue, which is important to the German; it causes the creative tension of debate. Any dialogue without debate is "small talk." Debate moves the dialogue towards a synthesis. Consensus requires compromise by both sides. Synthesis is seen as better than consensus. It is rather a new and higher level of truth which both sides see as a "new discovery."

Qualitatively, the dialectical approach is probably the most productive. It reinforces interdependence; it is creative. It is the stuff out of which symphonies are made: creative tensions leading to new forms of harmony. But this approach is the most difficult and time-consuming. Consequently, Americans don't like it.

The form of logic popular in France and Scandinavia is existential. It holds that facts in themselves are not adequate for reaching a conclusion. Communication cannot happen simply by using rational words. It ultimately happens on the irrational level of feeling, or emotion. For example, a man and wife don't make a home-buying decision simply on the basis of the house's location, size, and affordability. They must share the "gut feeling" that it is right. Feelings that confirm the decision-making process may come from things such as past experience, dreams, poetry, music, drama, aphorisms, parables, and metaphors.

We Americans attach little value to all this. Dialoguing to reach consensus again is too time-consuming. Dialectical logic is too stressful. Anything emotional is risky. And so we tend to make decisions independently and hastily. Should a wrong decision later cause damage, then we'll take the time needed to remedy it.

No one of these forms is better than the other. Jesus used all of them. He used linear when he said, "If you trust my heavenly Father, he will take care of you." He was contextual when he painted word-pictures of scenes familiar to his audience like sowing, fishing, and herding sheep. He was dialectical when he said, "You have heard that it was said, but I say unto you." His parables and miracles served to lead people through an existential experience of decision-making.

4. Styles of Leadership

The American leader tends to make decisions independently, and expects his subordinates to comply without raising too many questions. Koreans are probably more hierarchical (top-down authoritarian) than Americans. A Briton would be much more diplomatic in exercising her authority. A European would be inclined to consult with her subordinates towards reaching a leadership decision. Asians, especially Chinese, are more diplomatic than Europeans; hence more time is required to reach consensus. Australians have an anti-authoritarian stripe that tends to cut leaders down to size if they try to throw their weight around.[4]

One can anticipate the tensions these different leadership styles could generate in a multicultural missionary team. For example, an Australian would strongly react against being "bossed around" by a Korean leader. An American would become enormously frustrated with a Chinese leader who "wastes so much time" in coming to a consensus.

We have considered (1) approach to dialogue; (2) choice of words; (3) forms of logic; and (4) styles of leadership. Varying combinations of dynamics springing from these four areas can give rise to an infinite variety of potential conflicts.

Perhaps we could summarize basic principles for harmony in a multicultural team as follows:

1. Each member of the team must be aware of where every cross-cultural teammate is coming from, as regards the above four areas. Such knowledge must be applied towards analyzing and resolving misunderstandings as they occur.

2. Members must respect and affirm cultural behavior patterns of their peers that may appear strange, but are not in themselves wrong.

3. Manifest fruit of the Holy Spirit, particularly patience for times of misunderstanding, love as the bond that ties, and humility that enables one to say, "I'm sorry."

1. Campus Crusade for Christ has 5,112 fully supported national workers; Operation Mobilization has 600; Overseas Missionary Fellowship has 94; World Vision has 119; Latin America Mission has 22. For these and others, see: John A. Siewert and John A. Kenyon, *Mission Handbook: a Guide to USA/Canada Christian Ministries Overseas* (Monrovia: MARC, 1993- 1995 edition).

2. Sandra L. Mackin, "Multinational teams: smooth as silk, or rough as rawhide?" *Evangelical Missions Quarterly*, April 1992, p. 134.

3. For the following section I have drawn heavily upon a videotaped seminar lecture given by Kalevi Lehtinen, obtained from Agape International Training, P.O. Box 10389, Bakersfield, Calif. 93389.

4. Brian Butler, "Tensions in an international mission." *Evangelical Missions Quarterly*, October 1993, pp. 413-414.

5

Racism

Even missionaries, of all people, are not exempt from unrecognized racism. Once I operated a bookmobile in Zaire. It was a large closed van with an exterior display cupboard on its right side, an entry door in the back, and storage cupboards built along its inside walls, leaving a narrow aisle in the middle. My trained associate, Mr. M., and I travelled long distances, restocking bookstores, and selling to bystanders during roadstops.

We had restocked the last store, and were ready to make the four-hour trip to the city where we lived. Mr. M. asked if he could purchase a 50-gallon drum full of manioc, the African food staple, and haul it home with us. Manioc was much less costly here in the villages. I refused. We began the trip home.

"Why did you not allow me to bring manioc home with me?" he asked.

"It's still a long way home. I didn't feel we could take the time to buy it. Also, we'll be stopping several times along the way to sell books from the side cupboard. It would be difficult to get additional stock from the inside cupboards with that heavy drum filling the aisle. And the bouncy road ahead of us would cause the drum to shift; it would damage the storage cupboards' door latches."

After a pause, he replied quietly, "If I were a fellow missionary, you would have done it."

I didn't answer. But inwardly I was forced to admit that his remark bordered the truth. A fellow missionary, and Mr. M., weighed differently on my scales.

In another example, Mr. P., a church layman, was to move to our station. He was an experienced nurse, and would head up the station's medical work. One evening, three local African churchmen charged with finding housing for Mr. P. and his family convened a meeting with us.

Their question: Would Miss L. be willing to share her house with the single lady returning from furlough? Her house is plenty big for two persons. That would free up a residence for Mr. P. and his family.

Our reply: No. Over the years our mission has learned that single ladies function better if each has her separate living quarters. But in this case we knew it would not work—these two ladies could not get along living together.

One of those Africans and I were close friends. The next day he asked me privately, "Why are Americans upset with us Africans because our tribal divisions won't allow us to live in peace, when their single, lady missionaries can't live with each other? Or again, you taught us national church leaders that we should expect our believers to come to church and partake of communion whenever it is offered. Why is it that, when communion is offered here at church, the younger missionaries are absent time after time, and you say nothing to them about it?"

Again, we missionaries were measuring people by a double standard. Our attitudes were being shaped by remnants of racism.

Another time, our home mission board wanted to encourage the progress of evangelism programs on its overseas fields. It provided funds and the basic know-how for "Goals, Priorities, and Strategies Seminars" (GPS). It was a great idea. But implementing such a program in Zaire requires much more than jotting notes into an agenda book and making some phone calls.

On our field, we missionaries were training nationals to replace us. I had trained Rev. Boko in his responsibilities as director of the Department of Evangelism. I had ceded my leadership position to him, and now served alongside him as a "consultant."

To implement the GPS program in Zaire, Boko and I

would need to share the vision with the directors of evangelism from our church district centers. This would require that we call together 30 men from distances of up to 500 miles for three days of consultations. Roads were badly deteriorated; the only practical means of transportation was the mission's five-passenger plane.

That amount of flying would burn considerable fuel. Aviation fuel was expensive, costly to transport, and not always available. Eighteen months in advance Boko and I informed the pilot of our plans.

Eventually, the opening day of the consultation arrived. The program was scheduled to begin Tuesday at 2 p.m., but the sun was going down when the last planeload of delegates arrived; and Boko conducted the first session after dark.

Africans are not familiar with hearing presentations, having small-group discussions, and formulating conclusions within a given time frame. In spite of Boko's fine leadership, items scheduled for Wednesday before noon took the full day. Thursday morning began with the agenda item scheduled for 2 p.m. Wednesday. My anxiety began building about whether or not we would finish everything in the time allotted us. The pilot was coming at 4 p.m. Friday to begin shuttling delegates home. How would I explain it to the home board if we didn't finish our job?

The casual attitudes of three delegates heightened my stress. They were recognized leaders, but they seemed to be totally out of touch with the urgency of things. Both Wednesday and Thursday mornings, they came ambling to breakfast about the time the rest of us were finishing. They arrived at sessions late. Boko diplomatically urged that we all be punctual. They gave no heed. My pent-up frustration broke the dam. After Thursday's final presentation, I asked for the floor.

"Our Christian brothers in America have provided the money for us to do this work. We've been planning it for over a year. We have hoped this meeting will prove historical. Ten years from now, we want people to look back and say, 'At that GPS meeting in Zaire, they accomplished amazing things.' Now we are here. We have written two blackboards full of things we hope to do. But we can't come to the meetings on time. If we can't obey Director Boko and arrive on time while we are here, are we going to be serious about sharing all these things with others when we get back to our respective work places? Does this kind of attitude come from indifference, or from lack of comprehension?"

About six o'clock the next morning there was a knock on my bedroom door. It was Boko, still in his pajamas. I invited him in and showed him a chair. After some neutral conversation he said, "Some of our brothers came to me last night hurt by what you said about their coming late. Also, when you refer to your 'Christian brothers in America,' it suggests that we here in Zaire are not equally your Christian brothers. I think it would be good for you to make some remarks at the breakfast table about what you said."

When we had finished eating breakfast, I stood and apologized. I told them I was glad that they cared enough for me to reprimand me. If we were able to deal honestly with one another in this manner in the future, the progress in our evangelism program was assured. My apology was accepted; someone led us in prayer, and the issue was closed.

I pondered long on the above incident. What activated this pattern of behavior that strained my relationships with Africans? Learning patience has always proved one of my greater challenges. But this incident evidenced something beyond impatience.

First, if I had totally entrusted leadership of the department of evangelism to Pastor Boko, the problem of not keeping our time schedule at the consultation was not mine, but his. My decision to take the floor to reprimand people for tardiness was a clear sign to everybody that I had decided Boko had lost control of the situation, and that I alone could salvage it. To safeguard Boko's integrity before his peers, I should not have taken the floor. I should have dialogued privately with him about the problem later.

Second, my remarks to my African brethren in that situation showed that my posture towards them had not been as an adult to adults, but as an adult to children.

National leaders, freshly appointed by Caucasians to

positions of responsibility, have sensitive antennas tuned to pick up signals of racism. When we realize that they are reading the signals correctly, we must acknowledge our guilt, ask for forgiveness, and strengthen our resolve to monitor ourselves more closely.

On the other hand, nationals may resent our passing responsibilities onto them too hastily. One such leader whom I hold in high regard was appointed to the post of treasurer. I congratulated him on his appointment; I assured him of my faith in his abilities to fill the assignment. He replied, "Missionaries shouldn't give us such burden of responsibility too rapidly. We may feel your purpose is to make us stumble, so that you can point a finger at us and say, 'See. We told you that you're not yet ready to take over such duties.'"

Racism, in whatever form, always tends to debase the other person. It is an affront to God, the Creator of multiple races. To help me discern if my posture towards a cross-ethnic person is adult-to-adult, I might ask myself: Would I treat a fellow missionary in this manner? Would I feel comfortable if I were treated in this manner?

What can a young Caucasian person preparing for ministry in a cross-cultural setting do towards correcting unrecognized attitudes of racism?

Make friends with people of other cultures before going overseas. Invite them to your home. Interact with them on their own turf: visit their homes; share meals; participate in their ethnic celebrations; visit their places of worship. Try to find a cultural milieu similar to or identical with that of your anticipated field of service. Growing multiculturalism in North America makes such an experience increasingly possible. In large centers you can now immerse yourself in the activities of a community of Afro-Americans, or Latin Americans, or Muslims, or East Asians, or Chinese. Substantial interaction with people of other cultures should be a necessary component of cross-cultural missionary training.

Contacts with such persons can be made at their business places, in their markets, or on the sidewalks of their residential neighborhoods when people are at leisure. In most cases, such people are honored when they discover that we Americans want to learn more about their culture.

Some structure that provides guidance and requires accountability will accelerate the learning process. Sometimes this can be provided by a Christian service assignment, or by a faculty advisor. *Language Acquisition Made Practical* by E. Thomas Brewster and Elizabeth S. Brewster provides a very helpful method to follow for learning language and culture.[1]

When Eudene and I arrived on the field, the language-learning process seemed to us like traversing an arid desert. We felt alienated from the people because we couldn't talk with them. I discovered a time-proven axiom: Learning the language well at the outset opens the way to building deep and meaningful relationships for one's entire missionary career.

I found it very helpful to develop friendships on a deeper level with a few nationals—friendships strong enough to bear the weight of their constructive criticism. I can trust such a person enough to ask, "Would you help me by pointing out to me any times where my behavior is perceived by nationals as putting them down?"

Diligent efforts to get acquainted with cross-cultural people bring rich dividends. We will discover traditions that enrich us. We will recognize qualities of character that challenge us. We will treasure the gradual unfolding of a unique tapestry of relationships. When we come to know a people this well, little space will be left in the hidden recesses of our mind for remnants of unrecognized racism.

While each of us must work at our private agendas of correcting prejudicial attitudes, there is also need to focus our attention upon inequities that cause human pain and social dislocation on a much grander scale.

---

1. Published by Lingua House, 135 N. Oakland #114, Pasadena, Calif. 91182, Phone: (818) 584-5276. The course "Language and Culture Learning" is based on this book. Information on locations and dates of this course's instruction is also available at this address.

6

Living Among
the Poor

E udene and I were invited to visit believers at the village of Malanga for a weekend seminar of Bible study. About 40 adult believers and children, wanting to disentangle themselves from pagan customs practiced in the main village on the hill, had constructed their houses in two neat rows on a flat cleared area about half-a-mile distant, and closer to the main road. They welcomed us warmly, and provided us from the best of their limited resources for the weekend.

People were thirsty for instruction. They sat on their backless bamboo benches with open Bibles on their laps for two-hour sessions. After a Friday evening prayer meeting, Eudene and I retired to our cots set up in the mud-walled guest room of the parsonage. We learned that measles were ravaging the village's children. Inoculations are not available for the masses of children in Zaire's villages. Succeeding epidemics of smallpox, measles, and malaria cruelly controlled childhood population. Three of the pastor's children in a nearby room were ill, one of them in serious condition. We listened uneasily to their congestive breathing, until we finally fell asleep.

At four o'clock the next morning we were awakened by the voice of a woman wailing. At daybreak we learned that the 3-year-old son of a young Christian couple, their only child, had died of measles. We joined a cluster of Christians who sat with them at their home, sharing their grief for several hours. We held a brief funeral service and buried the body in mid-afternoon.

After the funeral the pastor and his assistant asked to see Eudene and me alone. "Thirty-six of our believers' children have measles. Unless God shows us mercy, there will be many other mournings and funerals. Parents are very worried about their children. They are looking to us leaders to do something. We've reached the end of ourselves. We're looking to you to help us."

After prayer, Eudene and I decided our only option was to apply the formula for healing outlined in James 5:14-16. We urged all parents who could come to meet in the chapel that evening. They came. After an explanation of the Scripture, we led in a time of penitent mutual confession of our sins. Then we asked for two saucers with a spoonful of palm oil in each.

Eudene and two church leaders took one saucer; two church leaders and I took the other. Eudene and her team began at the end of the first row of homes; my team and I began with the other row. We went from house to house, anointing, laying hands on, and praying for every sick child. We were shocked by their suffering and poverty. Sometimes we found four, five, or six children in a house. They lay on woven-reed mats on the dirt floor. A few of them were partially covered with pieces of faded cloth. Sweat beaded on their foreheads and coursed down their rib cages. Some were breathing short, raspy breaths. The homes had no furnishings as we know them; we didn't even see a blanket. We anointed and prayed over 36 children. God answered, and all 36 recovered.

This scene is a microcosm of how most people in today's world live. It reminds us of the gross disparity in the distribution of global wealth. My research discloses that 62 percent of the world's people live on less than $700 annual per capita income. In all likelihood, the vast majority of them have no access to either immunization against diseases, or even aspirin. Meanwhile, in North America, as a matter of course, one person spends $50,000 for a hip replacement, or $90,000 for heart bypass surgery. Recently $1 million was spent for experimental surgery on a pair of Siamese twins; one was sacrificed in the effort, and the other died.

How did we arrive at this point where we North Americans, 5 percent of the world's population, consume 45 percent of the world's natural resources?

In the late 1950s, carefully crafted manipulative TV and radio advertising launched us consumers on a spending binge. The media taught us that, contrary to what Jesus said in Luke 12:15, happiness *is* found in the abundance of our possessions. We have obeyed to the present, with a herd mentality, competing with one another to stay ahead.

For the younger middle-aged couple today, happiness is a spacious, lavishly furnished contemporary home with all the amenities of convenience and comfort, an ample wardrobe of fashionable clothing, a late model pickup (or van), an automobile, and a pack of credit cards.

For their teenage son or daughter, happiness means a closet full of name-brand clothing, a ghetto blaster, a CD player, a music library of cassettes or discs, a telephone, a TV, a VCR, recreational equipment, big stuffed animals, a bike and a helmet, and a shiny, sound-tight compact car or pickup with a high-powered stereo system.

People in Malanga have virtually none of these things. Could they in their wildest dreams imagine that there are people in the world who believe happiness can only be found in possessions?

What happens when a young woman from affluent North America goes to live among people like those at Malanga? If her testimony for Christ is to be credible, she must downsize her lifestyle.

How much should the missionary candidate downsize his or her lifestyle? There are those who believe that Jesus' lifestyle of total identification is the model for cross-cultural missionaries to follow. But in my experience, the few missionaries who have tried to match their lifestyles to that of Africa's poor masses have not been held in high regard by nationals themselves. While Jesus was poor, he did not will that people exist for all their earthly years with only the bare minimum of food and shelter necessary to support life.

Impoverished people are not looking for missionaries who imitate them; rather, they are looking for missionaries who model for them ambition, resourcefulness, hope, and a better way of life. How does the missionary make purchasing decisions that will help him or her fulfill this role model? Here are some suggestions.

Things you need that are available within the country should be purchased within the country; the local economy needs your help. Things you genuinely need that are not available within the country may be imported.

When you arrive on the field, you may discover that nationals you've come to serve live hand-to-mouth. Their limited earnings must all go towards purchasing food. This fact will powerfully shape your own eating habits. We purchased whatever vegetables we could at local markets or stores. We supplemented the variety by importing limited quantities of canned vegetables. All the fruit we needed was available locally. A pineapple garden we planted produced virtually year around. Rarely was fresh meat available. Africans around us had meat to eat less than once a week. We refused to import frozen meat from South Africa. The availability of peanuts and beans made meat less necessary.

Most household furnishings could be ordered from local carpenters. We purchased locally a lean-back chair and used it with a hassock, rather than import a Lazy-Boy. When we had four children, we imported a gas-motor powered washing machine. When our children left home, we sold it to another missionary family with children. We hired a house helper. He washed our clothing with a tub and washboard. We imported a kerosene-operated refrigerator, an item found in the homes of wealthier Africans.

A missionary colleague brought with him from the States a new portable stereo radio/cassette player. He enjoyed classical as well as Zairian music.[1] He could have reserved this "prestige item" for his personal use, and caused feelings of envy among local Africans. Instead, frequently he would set it on a chair in his front yard, tune it to a station with Zairian music, and turn the volume high. Sharing enjoyment of his stereo with his neighbors served to bond them to him.

What things should a missionary take to the field for enhancing ministry? A guitar? A pickup truck? A motor-cycle? A P.A. system? "While we have opportunity, let us do good to all men" (Gal. 6:10). The use of modern technology is part of our present opportunity. However, a program should never be developed in a manner that its survival depends upon the presence of expensive, imported equipment.

Take a pickup truck, for example. To do evangelism work we can walk, use public transportation (a bus or commercial truck), or ride in the missionary's pickup truck. If the pickup hauls the missionary, a pastor, a child evangelist, a medical staffperson, and a women's worker, then Christ's work is given impetus far beyond what could be accomplished on foot. To avoid fostering dependency, there should be a policy that persons riding in the pickup pay a fare, at a published rate, to help defray the truck's fuel and maintenance costs.

But a long-term program cannot be structured around availability of the missionary's pickup. So nationals should be shown how to use other forms of transport. Sometimes the ministry team (including the missionary) should use public transportation. Monies they customarily pay the missionary will now buy their fares on public vehicles. Sometimes they should leave the pickup at home and walk. Thus, should the pickup be removed, nationals have seen that ministry can continue without it. The missionary family owning the pickup should model that they are not totally dependent upon it for their personal mobility. Within reason, they should leave it at home and walk.

As with the radio/cassette player, the missionary should be prepared to share his or her pickup. Parents with a gravely ill child may request that the missionary take them to a distant hospital. A family whose relative has just died at the local clinic may request that the missionary transport them and the corpse to their home village. Charging for such services must be an established policy. The missionary should have a consistent policy regarding the use of his vehicle for such purposes, so as not to engender feelings of partiality.

Careful attention needs to be given to what happens with the vehicle when the missionary leaves on furlough. A private sales transaction with a progressive layperson may cause lasting hurt feelings with one's national superiors. Therefore, when the missionary first arrives with the truck, he should discuss openly with the local church council plans or intentions for the truck's final disposition. It might be sold on an agreed basis, the proceeds to be used towards the purchase of a new vehicle for the missionary's next term. Or, to preclude any accusations of partiality, the missionary might agree to contribute proceeds of its sale to the national church towards funding some specified project.

If you serve in a poor country, people will always perceive you as wealthy.[2] You come from the West which is wealthy. The church in the West pays for your living costs while you are there. This suggests that you have access to whatever they want. People will come to your door asking for things. How does one handle such requests? If people of the culture are very sociable (as Africans are), they may pay their first visits to become better acquainted with you. They are simply "checking you out." Frequently, at the end of considerable dialogue, they will present you with a "need." Your initial reaction may be to grant it; after all, you are anxious to build bridges to the people and to demonstrate that you love them. But unless people are destitute refugees, giving them whatever they need is not the best way to help them. Some needs are serious; some are not; some need to be met, but not by you.

You can patiently hear them out. Your undivided attention is in itself a gift. Understand that your gifts could never meet everybody's needs. Your gift to a person who is aggressive in his demands may foster ill will if you deny a person whose need is more acute, but whose presentation is less aggressive.

You can kindly say "No." You might respond as follows: "Thank you for coming to visit me. It shows me your friendship. I know that people here have many different kinds of needs. Your request is good. But I cannot grant it to you now. I need time to learn more about you and your culture. Whenever I give something, I want to know that I have been wise and fair in giving it."

You can say, "I cannot make a decision now." This will give you time to separate momentary impulse from a more objective evaluation of the request. Meanwhile, you can dialogue with missionary peers. You should become acquainted with the dynamics associated with gift-giving in that particular culture. You will build acquaintances by visiting people in their homes. At the point of request you can pray for the Holy Spirit's guidance. All of this will serve to increase your discernment skills about how to respond to people asking for your help.

Integral to living with the poor is the challenge to be fair and to do justice.

---

1. Missionary Gordon Klaassen, gifted in building positive relationships with Africans, was my primary source for the application section of this chapter.

2. For a definitive study on affluence as a Western missionary problem, see Jonathan J. Bonk, *Missions and Money.* (Maryknoll, N.Y.: Orbis Books, 1991).

7

Doing Justice

Once I was sitting in the church's pickup on a Zaire river bank, waiting to cross on a ferry. One of our Zairian church administrators, a close friend, sat between the African chauffeur and me. A soldier approached on my side and engaged me in conversation. He began pressuring me to give him a gift. (Soldiers frequently harass village people to extort gifts from them.) His remarks became intimidating.

I asked him, "Is it your duty to help people, or to torment them?" He remarked evasively about not wanting to cause trouble, and backed off.

Still waiting half an hour later, my attention was attracted by disorder. The soldier was gripping a large rooster in one hand, and fending off an angry village man with the other. The man reached for his rooster. The soldier threatened him. They began shouting at each other. Sullen-faced bystanders watched. The fracas was moving towards violence.

I got out of the truck, approached the soldier, and said, "Do you remember the question I asked you?"

"These people are stubborn. They don't want to listen."

"Did you pay the man for his rooster?"

"Yes. I paid him 20 Zs."

"Its price is 35," the man rejoined. "He's refusing to pay me more."

I knew that 35 Zs was a fair price.

"Do you have any more money?" I asked the soldier.

"Ten Zs."

"All right. Give the man 10 Zs. I'll pay the difference."

He did. I took a 5-Z bill from my billfold.

"Give it to me," the soldier said.

"No. I give it to the villager. It belongs to him. The transaction is closed."

Disgruntledly, the soldier with the rooster turned his back and left.

As we resumed our trip, my Zairian friend beside me said, "Yesterday at that ferry there was a fight; it was between soldiers and villagers crossing in a truck. People watching that argument today had already agreed that if the soldier continued harassing that village man, they were going to beat up on him."

This incident illustrates a definition of doing justice: acting out of compassion to help a needy person who cannot help him or herself. The supreme example of doing justice is the death of Jesus Christ. ". . . when we were still powerless, Christ died for the ungodly" (Rom. 5:6, NIV). Christ empowered us to be restored to our rightful place as children of God. If we are followers of Christ, we cannot escape our duty of doing justice.

Through most of its history, the church strongly committed itself to doing justice. It turned the value system of the Roman Empire upside down by insisting on justice in human relationships.[1]

1. Work

The Roman citizen took great pride in leisure. The only duties worthy of his time were politics, government, and military service. Work was despised and degrading; it blunted one's intelligence. Work was for slaves. Contrariwise, the Church Fathers proclaimed that idleness is a vice; it decays and ruins humanity. Christ was a carpenter. The apostles worked with their hands. Work, whatever kind, is honorable, praiseworthy, and suitable for all ranks of society. It provides the means for helping those less fortunate. This concept served to lift the despised and impoverished working people to a position of rank in society.

2. The Poor and Ill

The Roman saw the poor as despicable; their condition was unalterable. It was a virtue to deny them benevolence, because it would help them die the sooner. Sickness was worse than poverty; the ill were useless to the state, and hazardous to the healthy. They best be abandoned. Romans fled in panic from victims of epidemics.

Jesus ennobled the poor by being poor. He said, "To the poor the gospel is preached." In keeping with his spirit, the church embraced the poor. Charity and kindness to the poor were Christian duties. The church assured the poor a place in the kingdom of God. Christians directed their help to those who needed it most.

In the fourth century Lactantius said, "No one is poor before God but he who lacks justice; and no one is rich but he who abounds in virtues."[2]

Illness was even stronger reason for compassion. Jesus said those who visited the sick were visiting him. The Fathers made visiting the sick an imperative duty of all Christians. When persons were prevented by illness from gaining their livelihood, they were provided what they needed until they were on their feet again. Christians saw epidemics as opportunity to demonstrate their charity. They comforted the ill, brought them gifts, and carried the dead to the cemeteries.

3. Women

Laws confined women to an inferior status. They were disdained. Roman Statesman Metellus Numidious said, "If nature had allowed us to be without women, we should have been relieved of very troublesome companions."[3]

The Church Fathers restored to women the dignity accorded them in New Testament times. Widows were special objects of compassion. Soon women were making their mark in church history. They consoled prisoners, dressed the wounds of the tortured, prayed with martyrs, and showed themselves courageous as lions.

4. Children

Romans kept alive only those children that were robust and desired. Women disposed of unwanted children by abortion, or by exposing the newborn to death.

The church saw a child, from conception, as a gift of God's goodness. To take the life of a fetus was to murder; it destroys the work of God. All children were defended and protected, because "of such is the kingdom of God." Orphans, like the unborn, are defenseless. Bishops were charged with caring for orphans, nurturing their faith, teaching them useful trades, and placing them in families. Parents adopting orphans were encouraged to marry them to their own children, so that orphans would as soon as possible be encircled by their own families.

5. Slaves

Slaves were incapable of any virtue. They were tools without a will. Under threat of death, they were forced to fulfill the arrogant demands of their wealthy, effeminate, debauched masters: desires of toilet, eating, cleaning, bathing, sexual intercourse, sexual exhibitionism, recreation, or entertainment. Often a master, hosting a banquet, would require slaves to engage in gladiatorial combat during the meal, to delight his guests and to win their esteem.

The Church Fathers saw slaves as offering the highest form of charity. What greater love is there than to obey God and freely consecrate one's life to the service of others? Upon recognizing the principle of human equality before God, Christians began releasing their slaves.

In more recent centuries (1750-1950), European and North American missionaries campaigned against human injustices in their foreign fields of service. The tremendous social changes effected by missionary efforts are meticulously documented by James S. Dennis in his 630-page work *Christian Missions and Social Progress*.[4]

Missionaries protected native peoples from exploitation by governments and commercial companies. They combated forced labor, the opium trade, the exposure of babies, widow burning, infanticide, fetal marriage, temple prostitution, and the bondage of caste. Their efforts led to the abolition of slavery. They taught illiterates, healed the sick, cared for lepers, sheltered orphans, and restored other social outcasts.

> From the days of Las Casas in the New Spain to the days of the Anglican bishops in East Africa at the time of the forced labor ordinances, there has been a memorable succession of missionaries who were not afraid to fight their own governments, and to jeopardize their own comfort and reputation for the sake of what they understood to be justice to those for whom they could speak and who could not speak for themselves.[5]

If social justice was given a frontal position by the Early Church and foreign missions in the past, why has it been relegated to the back seat by many people involved in missions today?

For a combination of reasons. We are unaware of, or oblivious to, the biblical mandate for such action. For the most part, North American churches do not model such action for us. We don't need to include human rights in our evangelical agendas, because our national government addresses human rights on a global scale. The World Council of Churches makes social issues its primary concern. We don't want to risk the stigma of being "liberal." In a culture that lauds conformity, we don't want to "make waves" and be marked as some far-out cult. The risk of outright persecution isn't worth it.

These reasons and others comprise a formidable barrier. Are they enough to get us off the hook? No. Jesus directly confronted unjust men and their unjust systems, even if it meant feeding the animosity of those who wanted to destroy him (Matt. 23). His compassion for the downtrodden reflected the just character of God. We, the reconciled, have been given the ministry of reconciliation so that the world can be reconciled to God (2 Cor. 5:18-21). This can never happen so long as we, the reconciled, fail to speak for the powerless.

Perhaps a few examples of evangelicals who are currently involved in social justice issues will help us find a place to begin.[6]

● Since 1976, Caesar Molebatsi, a black from Soweto Township, South Africa, has been executive director of Youth Alive Ministries (YAM). For almost 30 years, the organization's weekly forums have given black youth opportunity to debate issues vital to them, and to evangelize by means of drama, music, and preaching. These forums have proved the training ground for thousands of articulate, well-informed black professional and civic leaders. YAM tutors students with special needs, instructs poor women on health, nutrition, and sewing, and feeds the impoverished. It seeks to develop holistic-minded Christians who can help transform society.

● Vinay Samuel with his wife, Colleen, resigned as senior pastor of a prestigious Episcopalian church in Bangalore, India. He felt the ecumenical patterns of social action distorted the gospel. He with his family relocated to live in a slum of 85,000, most of whom are Hindus and Muslims. He and Colleen organized a community development association (DSCA) with five areas of focus: school, child care, community development, economic development, and spiritual life, worship, and evangelism. DSCA has planted five congregations. Today it employs a paid staff of 250, and ministers to 50,000 people.

● In El Salvador, crushing poverty of the peasants spawned political unrest. Efforts of government forces to crush it caused a prolonged war that sent 500,000 people fleeing for refuge to the cities. Emmanuel Baptist Church (EBC), in the capitol city, moved to help them. With donor aid from the United States, the church began providing them with emergency food, water, and shelter. It requested a North American relief agency for personnel to come help with the people's long-term rehabilitation. Byron and Barbara Hiebert-Crape from Ohio answered the call. They arrived in El Salvador in 1990, and located in one specific area targeted by EBC for this mission.

Byron said, "The war was still raging. The people were in shock from the violence they had witnessed; they were afraid even to share their names. They were camping in garbage dumps, or along streams that were becoming sewers."[7]

Byron, Barbara, and an EBC pastor began to gather the peasants into small-group Bible studies. Gradually they shared their sufferings, and their struggles for day-to-day survival. This bonded them. From their Bible study they learned that every person is precious in God's sight. He loved them. They had identity. They could make decisions that would shape their future.

They began talking about things they wanted to do. They saw themselves as brothers and sisters working for a vision that would benefit them all. They started to take power into their own hands for the first time in their lives.

EBC leaders caught the vision of building a church. They acquired a plot on a steep hillside. The peasants brought hand tools, excavated the hillside and moved the dirt. Women and children, malnourished and in tattered clothing, carried sand, water, rebar, and concrete blocks on their heads over the top of the hill and down to the building site. The entire community, working together, built a retaining wall and a church. The building seats 500 and has space for other ministries. "It took an incredible amount of work," Byron marveled. "It was a miracle! When the building was dedicated, people from other city churches came and joined with them to celebrate."

As the result of further visioning, they have opened a clinic at the church, paid for the training of eight people to staff it, and employed them. Youth caught the vision; fellows formed soccer teams; girls formed softball teams. The best teams purchased uniforms and now play in city leagues. Byron and Barbara describe their four-year-term with these refugees as "the happiest period of our lives."

The process of giving a voice to the powerless does not always run so smoothly. Sometimes injustice is so deeply entrenched that such action becomes costly. Ricardo Esquivia, a Colombian lawyer whose work focuses on human rights, was falsely accused of murder. He took refuge in the United States until a government commission cleared his name.[8] Health worker Susan Classen led Bible studies in El Salvador, and was imprisoned for "teaching Marxist doctrine."[9]

How can an expatriate know when it is wise and when it is not wise to attack structured injustice? Judy Zimmerman, co-secretary for the Peace Office of the Mennonite Central Committee, replies, "Our overall guiding principle is to take our cues from the local people who can accurately interpret the situation for us. For example, in Brazil there is a movement of the landless peasants to reoccupy land taken over by powerful landlords. Local groups there said it would be very helpful for them if we, as expatriates, would publicize their plight. Appeals to our respective homeland governments would give their plight high profile and tend to restrain people in power over them from taking reprisal. On the other hand, when Mengistu ruled Ethiopia, church leaders were imprisoned. We would liked to have been more public about this injustice, but Ethiopian Christians said, 'Please don't; it would make more problems for us here.'"[10]

We may be inclined to say that doing justice in today's world is too complex, or too difficult, or too risky. But Jesus unhesitatingly gave his life to remedy the injustice of our eternal separation from God.

1. My primary resource for this section is C. Schmidt, *The Social Results of Early Christianity* (London: Sir Isaac Pitman and Sons Ltd. 1907).

2. Ibid., p. 28.

3. Ibid., p. 239

4. James S. Dennis, *Christian Missions and Social Progress* (New York: Fleming H. Revell Company 1899, 3 volumes)

5. Stephen Neill, *Colonialism and Christian Missions* (New York: McGraw-Hill, 1966), p. 415.

6. These examples have been selected from Ronald J. Sider, *Cup of Water, Bread of Life* (Grand Rapids: Zondervan, 1994).

7. Information gathered by personal interview.

8. "Year After Murder Accusation, Colombian Still Fearful." *Mennonite Weekly Review*, 21 July 1994, p. 1.

9. "My Work with the Poor is a Political Threat." *The Mennonite*, 10 October 1989, p. 478.

10. Mennonite Central Committee, 21 South 12th St., P. O. Box 500, Akron, Pa. 17501-0500.

8

Paternalism

Paternalism seeks to provide, without condition, all the needs of one's subordinates. An example is the over-protective father who, by an unbroken flow of giving, seeks to assure the total happiness of his child. Nothing so stifles the development of human dignity and self-reliance as paternalism.

Paternalism has plagued human wholeness in poor countries. It originated with colonialism. Western powers showered colonized peoples with unprecedented benevolences, a "compensation" for expropriating the colonies' natural resources to fuel Western industries.

I was a part of the colonial era. Belgium ruled Congo through its governor general who lived in the colony. The people of Congo enjoyed the patrimonies of Belgian rule: peace, stability, jobs, roads, schools, clinics, and stores. They did not recognize that they were being moved towards total dependency.

Regretfully, we missionaries, for the most part, identified with the power image of the colonizers. We collaborated with them. We felt it necessary; they welcomed us as "permanent guests" in "their" land. We, like them, came from the West. We dined each other. (Typically, the hostess would jingle a little silver bell, and a "boy" would come from the kitchen carrying bowls of hot, specially-prepared Western foods.) We gave them preferential treatment; they were white. We invited them into the house and offered them chairs. We talked with "natives" as they stood outside our screened office windows.

From its beginning, paternalistic attitudes transferred into matters of the church. Early missionaries enticed "natives" to attend church with gifts of salt, soap, and used clothing. Missionaries decided when believers could be baptized and who could partake of communion.

Significant administrative decisions were rarely left to nationals alone. Even in later pre-independence years, our mission policy reserved for the missionary alone the prestigious title of pastor. His national counterpart was the assistant pastor.

"One of the reasons for the shortage of clergy in Latin America and the Spanish-speaking communities of the United States is the conviction of the people themselves, engendered over the centuries, that the padre had to come from the 'outside,' from the 'superior outside.'"[1]

Paternalism, rooted in our own wrongdoing, persists to the present. It dogs our efforts to nurture self-dependency among formerly colonized peoples.

Example one: Zairians have a traditional history of keeping statistics in their heads rather than on paper. But Americans who give to the work of missions want to see progress. For them, progress is measured by printed statistics.

The time arrived for churches in Zaire to become autonomous. This meant that the task of keeping statistics must be transferred to our national counterparts. I prepared a basic set of forms to be completed. At a leaders' conference I painstakingly explained how to use the forms, and proposed dates for their submission. My efforts were met with unanimous disinterest. I asked if there were any questions. After an appropriate silence, a senior pastor asked, "Speaker, after we complete all this hard work, what will you pay us? Will you give me so much as a shirt?"

Example two: During one term of missionary service I was assigned to work in an area of specialized ministry. For this ministry to continue long-term, I needed to prepare an African to replace me. I began mentoring a gifted young married man. He was paid a regular salary. Occasionally he requested things; he was supporting a family. I provided him a 50-gallon drum for catching rain water, a large aluminum cooking pot, a selection of books from my library. I tutored him in English. I secured for him a salaried scholarship in a neighboring country whereby he could enhance his skills. As our furlough departure date approached, he asked me, "Isn't there one more little thing you can leave me as a souvenir?"

Example three: An American funding agency asked me to estimate the costs of holding a first-time-ever conference for all the denomination's pastors in Zaire. I itemized the estimated costs: food, lodging, honoraria, and travel (with gasoline at $10 a gallon), and submitted them. Later the agency wrote our denomination's Zairian church administrators. It offered to fund a five-day conference and give each pastor an allowance of six zaires for book purchases, on condition that each pastor pay three and one-half zaires towards covering his food costs.

The church administrators, all nationals, accepted the offer with enthusiasm. The church president sent pastors invitations, spelling out the condition. Ninety-eight delegates arrived. Many of them balked at paying their food fee. "We don't have that much money," they said. The president reduced the fee to three zaires. Still, many did not pay. The president said, "For those who aren't able to pay, we'll take three zaires from the six-zaire book purchase allowance."

At that point, those who had already paid their fees wanted reimbursements, allowing half the book allowance to cover their food fees as well. The president denied their request. A senior missionary took the floor and gave an instructive speech on the proper attitude required by beneficiaries of such a generous grant.

The Jewish philosopher Martin Buber has helped us understand how paternalism prevents the development of meaningful interpersonal relationships. He insists that most of us hold an "I-it" relationship towards other people. We do this to keep them at arm's length, so that we need not pay the costly price of personal involvement with them. However, our purpose for being is found in helping others, and a two-way flowing "I-thou" relationship is basic to any meaningful social experience. Only by this means can people constructively address one another's needs. Buber also points out that only by such two-way exchange can a person come to know himself as he really is. By consequence, a pattern of one-way giving can only dehumanize and alienate the person receiving our gifts.

How does such dehumanization manifest itself? As one might expect, it reveals itself in various forms of negative conduct. Such conduct affords the recipient a necessary outlet for his pent-up emotions of powerlessness and despair. The intensity of this negative conduct depends upon the degree of inner humiliation he suffers.

Here are five progressively intense forms of such conduct. First, when a recipient begins to recognize how one-way giving is affecting his personhood, he may resort to incredibly twisted logic in an effort to escape his sense of humiliation.

During the 1964 antigovernment rebellion in Congo's Kwilu Province, an important village chief led his people to join the insurgents. After his people suffered ghastly losses by war and deprivation, he withdrew them from the insurgent area to a place where missionaries could assist them with relief supplies.

One night he sat by a bonfire, silently pondering the events of past months. He had mistakenly led his people into great suffering. Now the necessity of relying upon the benevolence of others was a second blow to his personhood. Finally, he reasoned aloud, "My decision to lead my people to support the rebellion was a good thing. If I had not, we wouldn't be enjoying all the good things you are now giving us." His humiliation forced him to logic which would allow him to share the dignity of being a benefactor to his people.

Second, a stronger expression of the dehumanizing effects of giving is ingratitude. We had just moved into our newly constructed Congo home. Workmen mounted outside on scaffolds were painting its walls. A strange man came to the front porch and introduced himself.

"White man, I am traveling. Do you see my tattered

clothing? Could you give me a pair of trousers?"

"Yes, I think I may find a pair for you," I replied. "Meanwhile, would you mind doing a bit of work? Here is a rake. Why don't you rake this yard debris into a pile?"

Reluctantly, he took the rake and began to work. I entered the house, selected a pair of my jeans, and asked Eudene to cut off the legs and hem them. Thus the man would have a good serviceable pair of shorts, a pant-style common among Congolese men.

It took about 20 minutes for her to prepare them. During that time the man complained to me that he was tired, that it was getting late, that his journey was long. I gave the man his trousers and returned into the house. Shortly thereafter I heard workmen on the scaffolding guffawing.

"What's the matter?" I asked.

"The pants you made for that man? He went up the road a ways, threw them down, ground them into the dirt with his foot, and kicked them into the high grass."

This response reflected not only ingratitude, but bitterness and anger as well.

Third, dehumanization is frequently expressed in a more intense form by noisy, threatening demands for greater generosity. This may indicate that the person has been so dehumanized that he has lost all sense of self-dependence, and has abandoned hope of enjoying rightful personhood. He now sees himself as a disempowered entity, totally dependent upon his benefactor.

Frequently, refugees angrily protest that they are not getting sufficient relief supplies. At a northern Zaire relief center, Sudanese refugees struck for more food. When someone suggested that they should appreciate free food, one of them stood and said, "Well, maybe you Americans will be poor one day, and we'll be rich."[2]

This response could well reflect the refugee's effort to not lose grip on some final vestige of his personhood.

A fourth way of expressing the effects of dehumanization is thievery. If the benefactor has taken their personhood, they feel they have a right to take his things. So, what he understands as stealing, they feel is a justified form of expressing subdued revenge.

Finally, dehumanization finds its most intense form of expression by overt violence. The recipient, in order to alleviate his burning sense of injustice, may physically insult and reject his benefactor.

Frantz Fanon, the late Algerian psychiatrist, has profoundly analyzed the effects of colonialism upon the colonized in his work, *The Wretched of the Earth*. He contends that the colonialist handled the native not as a person but as a thing. He believed that this system so violently damaged the spirits of men that he justified counter violence as a "cathartic liberation of a demoralized and alienated people."[3] Such a view encouraged violent revolution against France to gain Algerian independence. Most developing countries, immediately after gaining their political independence, passed through an era of turbulence and disorder. Missionaries who were part of that history will recall occasions where nationals expressed these various forms of negative conduct.

The legacy of paternalism extends into the present. What can be done to help its victims recover dignity, self-dependence, and wholeness?

---

1. Louis J. Luzbetak, *The Church and Cultures: New Perspectives in Missiological Anthropology*, (Maryknoll, N.Y.: Orbis Books, 1988), p. 66.

2. John M. Jantzen, *The Etiquette of Charity: Forms of Giving and Receiving*, (Master's Thesis, McGill U., Montreal, 1970) p. 16.

3. Frantz Fanon, *The Wretched of the Earth*, (New York: Grove, 1965) as cited in Jantzen, p. 26.

9

From Dependency to Dignity

How can I help people whose dignity and potential are being denied them because of dependency arising from paternalistic giving?

First, I need to terminate any benevolence towards them that fosters dependence on me. This will give rise to accusations that "you don't love us any more." (In our part of Zaire, such disappointment was coined in a proverb of dismay, using the name of a missionary pioneer famous for his generosity: "Love died with Kuonyi Njila.")

Thoughtful Zairians today recognize the damage such giving has done. Recently a progressive church leader said, "You missionaries gave us too much. When I bought my car, pastors were begging me to provide them free transportation. I complied. Now the ones whom I helped most are among my strongest adversaries."

Second, I should help persons find means whereby they can begin to take ownership of their needs. This will help them discover the joy of empowerment that comes with self-reliance.

In Zaire, the husband clears ground for the family garden; then the wife tills the soil, plants and weeds the plot, and harvests the produce. A man with two small daughters came to my house. His wife had died. He had tuberculosis. Would I give him money for food? I complied. Later he came again; I complied. He came again. I needed to break the cycle.

His tubercular condition had not noticeably incapacitated him physically; with regular medication, it was curable. I determined that medication was available for him at the local clinic. I held him accountable to secure it regularly. I learned that a plot of ground was available for him to clear and till. I purchased a hoe and machete for him, and advised him that I wanted to come visit his garden plot, after he had planted the crops. There was no need for him to be shamed for doing the field work of a woman. Zairians have compassion for orphans, and would hold in esteem a man who violated custom to provide food for his motherless children. When his garden began to produce, he no longer needed gifts of money.

On a mission station where we once served, people coming to the local church gave generously. An established church accounting system had engendered their trust. Meanwhile, persons wanting gifts of money were wearing a path to the residences of benevolent missionaries. I asked the local pastor if I could speak with the church council about the need for Christians to care for the poor. He gladly complied. As a result, the church council recognized the need to take ownership of caring for the poor. It established a "box for the needy," and delegated a trusted deacon to take charge of it.

One-tenth of the weekly offering went into the box. Missionaries were instructed to no longer give money to persons coming to their door, but to direct such persons to the deacon charged with caring for the poor. He could better determine those persons who were genuinely in need. Missionaries were to give their monies either to the weekly church offering, or, if they preferred, as a designated gift directly to the deacon. He gave a monthly accounting of his receipts and disbursements to the church council.

This arrangement assured better stewardship of benevolence funds. It taught believers their biblical responsibility to the needy. It enhanced the self-worth of the church council by taking ownership of its responsibility. It lifted off of missionaries' shoulders a burden which primarily was not theirs to bear.

Glenn Schwartz, director of World Mission Associates, Reading, England, an organization specializing in issues of dependency and self-reliance, tells about a young African pastor who worked for a North American relief and development agency. He lived in the capital of the country where the organization was seeking to provide food for villagers who did not have a good harvest. The pastor asked the leaders of the agency, "How much do you expect our local people to give towards this drought relief project? After all, the people suffering out in the rural areas are the relatives of those of us who live in the towns. It is our privilege and responsibility to be the first to be asked to help." He was told that the agency had a monthly quota to be given away. If it was not, the quota from overseas would be reduced the next month.

The young pastor decided to quit promoting local support for the project. Schwartz says that what happened to that young African is symptomatic of what lies behind the syndrome of dependency in many places where well-meaning Westerners try to help.[1]

On the other hand, the leader of a denomination in South Africa, while on a fund-raising trip to the United States, responded to God's word to him that he should not get the money for his church there, but from his own people. At the annual assembly the people gave more than $700,000. When the women made 10 mats, they set aside one for the offering; 20 baskets, two for the church; 30 dresses, three for the assembly.[2]

In recent years, Christian development agencies have made special efforts to design aid programs in a manner that fosters people's dignity and self-worth. We who seek to discourage paternalism in our relationships can learn from the programs of such agencies.

One example is the strategy of Medical Ambassadors International (MAI), in existence for two decades, and now active in 19 poorer countries.[3]

The initiators of an MAI program in a given rural area are a team of trainers, minimally a pastor, a medical person, and an agriculturalist. The training team is organized and prepared by the national director of MAI and an expatriate representative from the home base in California. MAI pays each member of the training team a stipend to cover basic living costs for him and his family, because his responsibilities keep him away from home for much of the time.

The team of trainers, normally accompanied by a local pastor, visits the village chief. They explain to him the program they offer: "We show your fathers and mothers what they can do so that they and their children will have better health. We can help you increase the harvests from your fields. We want to teach you about Jesus Christ, the healer of our bodies and souls."

If the chief is interested, he calls a meeting of all the people. There the program is explained in detail. If the villages choose to adopt the program, they appoint a local committee of 15 to 20 people. The committee divides the village into areas of 20 to 40 families each. It appoints a trusted, mature person to serve as a Community Health Evangelist (CHE) in each of these areas. The training team requires that CHE appointees:

1. attend intense training sessions two or three afternoons a week for a period of four to six months;
2. model by their own lives what they learn;
3. have their own fields;
4. give one day a week to teach what they have learned to families in their respective areas;
5. report their activities once a month to the village committee;
6. serve without remuneration.

To implement the program, the training team begins regularly scheduled training sessions for the CHEs. They are given all the needed instructional materials. The team teaches them a series of simple lessons in preventative medicine, agriculture, and personal evangelism. It sends them to do practical work assignments in their respective village areas. Normally the assignment of a CHE will be to teach his or her area a social and a spiritual lesson; perhaps, "How to keep a clean kitchen," and "The origin of sin." After the CHEs have completed their work assignments, they meet with the team and dialogue about their experiences.

By the end of their training period, their practical work experience has provided them self-motivation. At this time the training team invites the entire village to attend a graduation ceremony where the CHEs are honored, and are awarded certificates. At that point, the village committee takes responsibility for supervising the project. It forwards monthly reports of the CHEs activities to the training team which is meanwhile introducing the MAI program into other villages. The training team encourages village CHEs by returning occasionally to give them refresher courses. The regular weekly teaching activities of the CHEs empowers people to take ownership of life issues on a personal level.

One training session is devoted to choosing a village project. The training team asks each CHE to hunt for one object which represents a common need that the village people and MAI can work together towards accomplishing. The CHE is to return with this object, and three leaves.

When they reassemble, each CHE in turn, lays his or her object on the ground and explains the need it represents: a water source, a school building, a medical clinic, literacy classes, fertilizer for their communal field, or whatever. Then the CHEs vote by placing their three leaves by the projects they feel are most needed. Then the training team and the CHEs, in collaboration with their villagers, discuss the three projects receiving the most votes, and decide which one they wish to undertake together, first.

For example, where a water source requires damming a stream, MAI might provide two bags of cement; the villagers would provide three bags of cement, carry all the sand and gravel needed, hire persons knowledgeable in dam design and masonry to construct it, and volunteer unskilled labor.

A communal field tilled by members of the village committee empowers them to address a need corporately. The CHEs help the committee members decide where the field is to be located, and those days when they will go together to work in the field. This project generates community spirit and enhances self-worth. It inspires individuals to plant personal gardens around the periphery of the communal plot. Produce is sold, and the proceeds are used to accomplish their previously determined project.

Notice how the strategy of MAI is in keeping with Martin Buber's principle related in the previous chapter. It avoids one-way giving which fosters an "I-it" relationship. Instead, it enters into the world of needy people, and by sharing their burden, develops a wholesome "I-thou" relationship that leads them towards wholeness of personhood. Thus, people recover dignity, and discover empowerment. They will turn their back on any subsequent paternalistic benevolences.

French ethnologist Marcel Mauss tried to determine why one kind of giving leaves a man in another's debt, disgracing and humiliating him like a bondslave, while another kind of giving raises him to the dignity of genuine personhood. From his study, Mauss formulated what he believed is an inviolable principle: that giving puts in motion a rule by which the thing received is obligatorily returned in kind or intention.[4]

Dr. John Janzen, a Christian anthropologist who did his doctoral studies in the Congo, says, "Wherever generosity of giving, teaching, and helping is of an unconditional character, the recipient must be able to return the gift or some equivalent in order to remain his own respectable self. Otherwise, he will begin seeing himself as inferior to the giver; his personal sense of worth is downgraded, and instead of being grateful, he will be bitter. This set of forces is very much misunderstood in many missions programs today."[5]

Suppose that you, by means of a gift, address an important need in the life of one less fortunate than yourself. Following the above principle, you could help such a person maintain self-respect by suggesting that someday he or she might find occasion to reciprocate the favor. You must be prepared to receive with thanksgiving whatever gift your beneficiary offers. In Zaire this could be produce from a field, two eggs, a pigeon, or being made hero for a day by a big village feast.

For example, while living in a large city in Zaire, I frequently conducted Sunday services in the provincial prison. On one such occasion I met a man from a distant tribal area where I had once lived. He had been involved in the tumultuous events connected with the coming of political independence, and was arrested on a murder charge. He was imprisoned, and apparently forgotten. Now, two years later, he pleaded that I bring his case to the attention of the authorities.

I visited the government's prosecuting attorney. He checked the files and could find no record of this prisoner's case. Inasmuch as there was no reason for detaining the man, the attorney issued an order for his release. Later at my home the man told me, "Speaker, if God hadn't put love in your heart, I'd have stayed in that place forgotten forever." I suggested that someday when I arrived at his village, we might have a feast of celebration.

He didn't wait. Some weeks later a stranger arrived at my home in the city. It was my friend's representative. This man had ridden in the open beds of trucks over rough roads for a distance of more than 200 miles to deliver my gift: a live pig.

In another example, a Zairian chief came to a missionary doctor to ask for glasses. But the thought of how a gift of glasses would indebt him to the doctor threatened his sense of personal integrity. So he was reluctant to make an outright request. After lengthy causal visiting, the doctor came to understand the problem. So he asked the chief to do him a favor. The chief consented. This opened the way for the chief to ask the doctor for a favor in return: a pair of glasses.[6]

You may ask, Didn't Jesus say to give, expecting nothing in return (Lk. 6:30ff)? How is it that you say we should give, and suggest reciprocation? It seems to me Jesus warned us against a kind of giving that has a selfish motive hidden within it; a kind of giving that is generous only because I expect something in return: a posted bronze plaque, or an identifying name-plate; a kind of giving which is a subtle form of self-serving. He sternly rebuked people for this kind of "showmanship giving" (Matt. 6).

If I suggest the person give me something in return, it is not to memorialize myself. Rather, it is to help preserve the person's dignity and self-worth. A woman of ill repute expressed her love and gratitude for Jesus by washing his feet with her hair in public. Jesus praised and affirmed her (Lk. 7:36-48). Jesus' giving was never self-serving. His entire public ministry was an abandoned giving of himself to others, in a manner that made them completely whole.

How fraught with potential is a gift! How awesome the responsibility of Western missionaries who serve among less-privileged people! Our well-intentioned efforts to help can either violate people's right to wholeness by perpetuating their dependency, or can free and empower them, restoring dignity to them.

1. *Transition Notes*, World Mission Associates, Reading, England, November, 1995.

2. *Evangelical Missions Quarterly*, January, 1994, p. 36.

3. Medical Ambassadors International, P.O. Box 576645, Modesto, Calif. 95357-6645.

4. Marcel Mauss, *Essai sur le Don* (Paris: University of France, 1960).

5. Jantzen, op. cit., p. 16.

6. Ibid., p. 14.

10

Financial Management

When a national church becomes autonomous, nationals must assume responsibility not only for directing the church, but also for directing programs inherited from its founding mission. Such programs may include hospitals, rural clinics, schools, printing presses, guest houses, orphanages, programs of Scripture translation, literacy and literature development, agricultural and community development, and preventive health care.

Skilled persons from Western industrialized nations take leadership of such enterprises as a matter of course. But nationals given those positions of leadership have found their tasks overwhelming. They must cope with powerful interwoven cultural dynamics of which we from the West are largely oblivious.

A mission station was established in Central Africa. The area was populated with one primary tribe comprised of two clans (Clan A and Clan B), and with a few smaller tribes. In the course of time, well-qualified missionaries established an agricultural development program. The mission hoped to increase the protein in local diets so as to improve people's health; and to lift their standard of living so they could better support their church.

To achieve the above goals, missionaries imported good breed baby chicks, rabbits, and wire netting for cages. Chickens and rabbits were small enough for a family to eat without requiring refrigeration, and were easy to care for.

The program proved successful. Raising rabbits or better-breed chickens became a status symbol among Africans living at the mission station, and in a wide range of villages around it. Church offerings increased, and maintained a level considerably higher than elsewhere.

The time came for the missionary director to transfer his responsibilities to an African. The administrative committee charged with finding the missionary's replacement chose Mr. T., a highly respected layman of Clan A, with a wife and three young children. For many years he had worked alongside the missionary director.

The choice of Mr. T. was a point of honor for his family and clan. He was committed to proving that he was worthy of his assignment. He began his duties. His missionary mentor left for furlough.

From time to time, a member of Mr. T.'s extended family would visit him, asking for a special favor—a rabbit, a small piece of chicken wire. They were denied it. This angered them. In time, Mr. T. was visited privately by three elders of his extended family.

"Because you sit in the directorship chair, you are a person of much wealth," the spokesman said. "When you get old, and no longer sit in this chair, who is going to take care of you?"

Mr. T. knew that the mission could not provide social security benefits for its national retirees. "I expect that my extended family will provide for my needs, as is our custom," he replied.

An elder fastened slitted eyes upon him. "You know that we always care for one another. If you, with wealth in your hands, don't start taking care of us now, don't expect us to take care of you when this job ends."

Mr. T. did not want to be accused of discrimination. By design, he made sure that Clan B was generously represented among his employees. To Mr. T.'s clansmen, this suggested betrayal of his own clan's interests. They were also disappointed that he did not use his position to collect and display the status symbols characteristic of a chief; such symbols earn the esteem of a chief's people.

From that point, his extended family and clan began snubbing him. But neither were people of Clan B happy. Rumors of uncertain origin began to circulate:

"Where is Mr. T.'s father getting all his wire netting?" "How is it that people of Clan A are getting so many rabbits?"

"Did you see Mr. T. when he went to the big city last Friday? He had 16 chickens in the back of the pickup; that money went into his pocket."

"Look! Mr. T. is putting glass windows in his house! How can he afford to do that, while the rest of us remain poor?"

One weekday morning, in the church on the mission station, a man from Clan B who worked under Mr. T. rose to bring the daily chapel message. He chose his text from Matthew 22:37-38: "O Jerusalem, Jerusalem, you who kill the prophets and stone those sent to you, how often I have longed to gather your children together, as a hen gathers her chicks under her wings, but you were not willing. Look, your house is left to you desolate." Then he told a parable.

"Once upon a time, a parrot and a canary lived near a village. They agreed to go hunting together. The canary shot an animal. The parrot squawked, 'I shot it! I shot it!' The village people came, and praised the parrot.

"The canary and parrot went hunting a second time. The canary shot an animal. Again, the parrot squawked, 'I shot it! I shot it!' Again, the village people came, and praised the parrot.

"The canary and parrot went hunting a third time. Again, the same thing happened; the parrot loudly squawked and got the credit; the canary was ignored.

"When they went hunting the fourth time, the canary saw through the bushes a moving object. He shot. Again, the parrot squawked, taking credit. The canary discovered he had killed a man, and fled. The parrot arrived at the body. The villagers found him there. They cut his head off."

Everyone in the audience immediately understood the intended message: We people in Clan B are doing all the hard work; Mr. T., of Clan A, is taking all the credit. The day is coming when Mr. T. will make a misjudgment, and will be put to shame before everybody. (The story also could be taken as a hint that Mr. T. might be killed by witchcraft.)

Meanwhile, short-term American service workers who supervised the overall functioning of development programs of the mission's entire geographic area held a retreat. From reports brought to them, they concluded that "the worst exploitation is being done by the development programs' national directors themselves." This opinion reached the ears of the senior missionary living on the station with Mr. T. Now he felt compelled to visit Mr. T. "If the axe falls, and he is proven guilty of mismanagement," the missionary reasoned, " I don't want him to feel I failed to support him in his time of testing." One morning the missionary arrived at Mr. T.'s office. Mr. T. stood, smiled, shook his hand in greeting, and asked him to sit down. After some casual dialogue, the missionary addressed the issue.

"I know these are very difficult days for you. You are carrying a heavy load. I want to encourage you. The mission establishes agricultural development programs to help people rise above a hand-to-mouth existence. It wants to help correct injustice in our world. Some people use their power to become rich, and exploit the poor. The biggest peril to our development programs is that a director himself would capitulate to covetousness, take bribes to show favoritism, or take things which are not his. Then he himself is the exploiter. These days there is a lot of smoke in the air. When the smoke clears, may people see plainly that you yourself have not set any of the fires. I encourage you to keep good records of all your transactions. Be transparent and honest in your dealings. Don't do anything that you need to hide. If you feel that counsel from any of us missionaries might be helpful, please consult us." Mr. T. thanked the missionary for his visit. The missionary prayed with him, and left.

Mr. T. pondered his situation. "My extended family abandons me. My clan accuses me of discrimination in hiring. It says I am a chief without glory, a chief who brings them shame. Workers of Clan B are jealous of my position.

They publicly predict the day of my downfall. They even hint using witchcraft to eliminate me. Now the missionaries themselves suspect me of unfaithfulness. Who believes in me? How can I make anybody happy? My wife, my children and I are left standing alone. How much longer can I bear up under this? How will it all end?"

Mr. T.'s missionary mentor returned from furlough. People rushed to him with complaints against Mr. T. They begged the missionary to reassume directorship of the development program. Accusations mounted against the development program's administrative committee that it was ignoring a volatile crisis. The committee set a date when inventory of the development program's assets would be taken. Then Mr. T.'s status would be reviewed.

The inventory was taken. It showed a negligible deficit. The Committee, seeking to appear impartial, relocated the agriculture missionary to another station to start a program there. It replaced Mr. T. with a first-term missionary, and put Mr. T. in charge of a new program—establishing small-scale development programs in area villages (a move everybody viewed as a demotion).

Why could Mr. T. not manage a development program? The answer is not "tribalism." That is an oversimplification. Traditional African culture was highly developed. Over the centuries it had been shaped to suit perfectly the needs of those who owned it. As with any culture, it has its own value system and expectations. We of the highly developed West have sought to impose upon Africans our own culture with its very different expectations. When their value system stubbornly refuses yielding to our own, we too readily conclude that their "primitive culture" is "obstructing progress."

Mr. T. could not manage the program because of two irreconcilable value systems. Before the arrival of the white man, Africans had no money.[1] As regards economics, there was nothing to save, nothing to manage. Europeans brought them money, and with it, the ability to accumulate wealth, the introduction of class structure, the power to exploit, and the fertilization of jealously and greed. Traditional African culture moved in rhythm with the sun, the moon, the seasons. European culture introduced the need for time keeping, schedules, deadlines, and goals.

The primary concern in African culture has been self-preservation. Life was too precarious to risk change. The concept of progress had not occurred to them; it met none of their felt needs. When the concept was introduced by Europeans, it radically disrupted the Africans' psychological environment of security and predictability.

The Africans' common struggle for survival did not allow for the luxury of individual ownership. Ownership was communal; sharing was mutual. This fostered group solidarity; it fostered bonding on a level deeper than oral and written pledges. Europeans introduced "free competition" which taught that a person could make a one-time payment of money, and thereby claim exclusive ownership of something, putting it "off grounds" to anybody else. This ruptured bonding, eroded group solidarity, and served to pit person against person.

African culture is socialistic. It attaches high value to dialogue and consensus, to interpersonal relationships, and to the well-being of each individual. Western culture is highly individualistic. Deep relationships are secondary. People are expendable for the success of a program.

Is the African value system "inferior" to ours? No one is qualified to make such a judgment. None of us is impartial, because all of us are attached to a value system.

But it is clear that no country can be a part of global modernization without development; and development necessitates that somebody manage corporate assets on behalf of others. What qualifications does a non-Western person need to succeed in a position like that of Mr. T.?

The role of Mr. T. could have been better filled by a qualified person from one of the minor tribes of the area. Such a person would be motivated to do his job well, to raise the perceived status of his tribe. Neither clan of the main tribe could lay any claim upon him.

For a more complete answer to the above question, I asked Africans who themselves have capably filled such roles.

A progressive businessman: Such a person should be already well-established financially. Then, when a brother or family elder comes demanding that he help them by sharing his wealth, he has an alternative source to dip into. The wealth of outsiders with which he has been entrusted can remain intact. Also, he maintains the respect of his extended family.

Those appointing the candidate must be in agreement that he genuinely loves the work he is being chosen to lead, that he is not feigning love for it in order to get his hands on a source of cash.

Before he accepts the position, those over him should establish a schedule of regular inventories to be taken, so that he knows he is always being held accountable. Otherwise, an inventory sprung upon him unexpectedly tells him that his superiors have already begun to mistrust him.

When an inventory discloses that he has embezzled funds, plans for repayment must be made immediately. Otherwise, he is ruining benefits of the program for everybody. If he fails to keep on schedule with repayment of the funds, he should not be discarded. He should be given less responsible work, and still required to repay all that he embezzled. This way he is helped as a person, his honor can be restored, and everybody recognizes that he made no financial gain by his misconduct.

A successful construction contractor: My father paid my way to get a trade-school diploma, but he never taught me to work under discipline. I learned that later, in Switzerland, when I was forced to be a lowly mason's helper alongside illiterates, freezing in blowing snow, having no way of escape. There I learned submission to authority, and obedience. This gave me pride, not for cleverness in mishandling funds, but pride which comes with professional accomplishment. As my hard work and integrity gained me promotions, my professional accomplishments became a matter of personal honor. Maintaining my honor became far more important to me than any supposed benefit from exploiting persons or monies entrusted to me. Accountability by means of an inventory is not intimidating;

rather, it is welcomed as an opportunity to show everybody that I am capable of doing the job entrusted to me. Work closely with a person who shows promise. Insist that he do his job well. Pass responsibility on to him bit by bit. Keep holding him accountable. After two or three years you will see him develop a real thirst for his work, and a genuine interest in its long-term future.

A senator in the national parliament: It is very difficult for a person of purely African culture and experience to serve the larger community or nation. You ask, Why? As little children we are taught that stealing from somebody of our tribe is wrong, but stealing from someone from another tribe is good, because what you steal will benefit all of us. This causes tribes to suspect each other rather than to trust one another. This is a major problem we struggle with in government all the time. Politicians from different tribes are unable to trust each other. Because Africa is a tribal society, this is a problem for all of Africa. I believe it is one of the reasons why Egypt, one of the world's most ancient civilizations, is still among the world's poorest nations.

This will be a problem for us until our children in primary school learn values that are essential to living as part of a global community: to love and trust and serve beyond tribal boundaries. Meanwhile, in spite of this difficulty, we do what is necessary to enable us to function. For example, I am treasurer of a large church. The money is kept in the bank. I have charged one person with making all the deposits, and another with making all withdrawals, and I alone sign for the transactions.[2]

Churches in Africa face a challenge: what they should or should not adopt from Western culture. Meanwhile, the church in the West faces an enormous challenge it has hitherto ignored: the Muslim world.

---

1. For this summary of contrasts between African and Western value systems, I am indebted to Dr. Dan Fountain, a missionary of the American Baptist Foreign Missionary Society of Zaire.

2. Leading African writers reflect on the fusion of African culture and Western Christian beliefs in *African Spirituality*, by Aylward Shorter, editor, (Maryknoll, N.Y.: Orbis Books, 1987).

11

Imprisonment

*T*he following is a true account, with names changed and sensitive facts modified for reasons of security. Ernie Chalmers tells his story:
Dianne and I checked our baggage. She held three-month old Andrew, and I held our air tickets. Our hand luggage lay at our feet. We'd been planning seven years for this. About 50 friends had come to the airport to see us off. It was a highly emotional moment. This was our first term of overseas service. Our destination was a Muslim country with a government hostile to Christianity. Someone led our group in prayer. Then we hugged, choked up, smiled, waved goodbye, and went on board. Doors slammed shut, and the plane climbed steeply into the night sky.

I leaned my seat back for comfort. Why should I feel apprehensive? We had laid plans carefully. Our team leader, Tim, had been living in the country for three years. Dianne and I would be joining four other couples already working there. All of us were bivocational missionaries. The country readily granted "business" visas. We operated a business that was set up to import useful products into the country, and to provide opportunities for sharing our faith. Dianne and I had studied Bible and missions. I had a degree in business and a year of experience. Our U.S. sponsoring agency had used the "team" approach for many years in many countries. It had yet to encounter serious difficulty with government authorities.

Our host country was considered moderately Muslim. It had signed the U.N. Charter of Human Rights. That declaration guarantees freedom of religion, freedom of worship, freedom to teach religion, and freedom to change one's religion. I was grateful that God had called Dianne and me to serve in the most gospel-deprived area of the world. Apprehensive? Yes.

But I'd never felt better.

We arrived at the capital city and settled into a third-floor apartment. Then Tim, our team leader, began orienting us. He required five conditions of persons joining the team:

1. at least five years in the Christian faith;
2. a love for Muslims;
3. a willingness to suffer;
4. a willingness to learn;
5. submission to the team leader's authority.

"We aren't here to convert Muslims to Christianity," Tim explained. "We are here to persuade Muslims to become followers of Jesus Christ. A Muslim who decides to follow Christ does not need to extract himself from his Muslim culture or his community. In fact, we encourage converts to continue those Muslim traditions which are not incompatible with the Bible. We as team members try to identify with the culture here by adopting these customs ourselves; they can serve to deepen our own spirituality. Our wives dress like Muslim women; that clearly sets us apart from the 30,000 or so Americans here. We have the challenge of modeling for them what we understand a Muslim believer should look like."

Dianne and I rapidly blended our gifts with those of the team. Soon it became clear that my niche was evangelism. I gave most of my time to developing relationships and planting churches.

People were unusually hospitable. I would practice simple Arabic sentences in the street. Soon a friend would invite my wife and me to his home for a meal. He would have his family and friends there to meet us. Invariably, the conversation would turn to the subject of religion. This would open the way for Dianne and me to invite them to our home for a meal and to watch the "Jesus" film. They would accept and come. After the film, we would get into lengthy, meaningful dialogue. We had such in-home encounters four or five evenings a week.

By the seventh month I was witnessing to at least one person daily. New converts averaged about one a week; nationals were discipling them one-on-one. We had 45 baptized believers; no one had lost his job because of his beliefs. Asharof, a young man from a highly respected family, had been converted about two and one-half years earlier. He'd been incarcerated in a mental hospital for a time because of his faith, but he remained steadfast. He is a gifted evangelist, and was emerging as the leader of our small "house church" that met in our home Thursday evenings. Our weekly meeting was now a powerful witness to other people in the apartment building. One evening I wrote my dad saying, "With all the attacks Muslim Fundamentalists are making on Western tourists, the last thing this government wants to do is throw a Westerner in jail." I went to bed like on any other night, and slept.

Something awakened me. It was the doorbell. I turned on the light: 5:30 a.m. Only some major problem in the building or the police would arouse us at such a time. I went to the door. My heart was pounding.

"Who is it?" I asked.

"Mr. Chalmers, this is the police. We would like to come in."

"Let me get dressed first."

"All right."

While dressing I asked myself, Should I try to hide things? In the clutter on my office desk was a letter I'd prepared for our supporters. It detailed all of our accomplishments here to date and revealed other delicate information. No; any delay would heighten their suspicions. I went and opened the door. There stood six plain-clothed officers and two armed policemen.

Instantly they fanned throughout the apartment searching. One of them went to my office and turned on the light switch; that moment the bulb burned out. They took whatever they could see: my briefcase, my stock of Arab Bibles, all the papers off my desk. They missed my letter file and computer disks, thank God. They took me into the hall.

"You need to go with us downtown for questioning. It's a routine thing. Tell your wife not to worry; you'll be home by noon."

We drove downtown. I was shocked when the truck hauled us through the iron gates of the high-walled yard of Secret Police headquarters. This is the building to which arrested Islamic Fundamentalists are taken for interrogation.

An armed guard took me to the third floor, then to the end of a long corridor, and told me to sit on the floor. I sat there for about two hours. I felt an evil, oppressive presence. When the guard took me back downstairs to the restroom, I glanced into an office and saw Asharof, our house church leader.

Later they brought Asharof, blindfolded and handcuffed, up into the corridor with me. They left him standing about eight feet away. He stretched out his arms, groping for a wall. I feared what might be in store for him. To comfort him, I began humming one of the songs we sang at our home fellowship. Later they came and took him away.

They took me into an office. An Arab with jet-black hair and a navy-blue blazer sat behind his desk. He harangued and harassed me for what seemed like a long time. Eventually I was taken to a holding cell. Later they brought Tim, our team leader; then, Bill, another team member; then Ned, also a Western bivocational missionary: we were four Caucasians. That night a guard awakened us about every half hour.

The next day they took me to the Court House for interrogation. The district attorney (D.A.) would ask a question in Arabic; a man whose English was poorer than my Arabic translated it to me; I answered. The translator told the D.A. in Arabic, and the D.A. dictated to the stenographer what to write.

"Did you try to convert Muslims to Christianity?"

"No."

"Do you want Muslims to become Christians?"

"We never desire for Muslims to become Christians. I have a strong desire for Muslims to follow Jesus Christ."

Eventually the D.A. asked me to sign the transcript. I refused, without knowing what they had written.

They got Asharof. He read it to me in English. It was a mixture of truth, misunderstandings, and lies. I made them rewrite much of what they had written; then I signed it. They returned me to the holding cell, and took Asharof elsewhere.

We wanted to encourage Asharof. We bribed some guards to allow us to see him. We gave him our one English New Testament, and prayed with him. He was becoming depressed; he feared for his future.

The second day passed. We'd had neither food nor water. We bribed a guard to bring us a chicken sandwich. Again, that night, they did not allow us to sleep.

About noon of the third day they took the four of us from the holding cell and loaded us into a closed-bed truck with a small window on either side. Normally, foreigners in trouble were hauled to the airport and deported. Instead, they hauled us to the Central Prison. I'd heard how foreign prisoners were abused in such places. I felt my heart pounding; my hands shook. They took us inside into an office and introduced us to the warden. Among other things, he said, "Muslim fundamentalists are in there; if they know why you are here, they won't think twice about killing you." Guards gave us each a blanket, took us inside a prison ward, and showed us to a bare cell. I sat down on the floor against a wall and wept.

Other prisoners clustered around us.

"Why are you here?" they asked.

"We don't know."

Immediately, they set their minds to making us more comfortable. They brought us mattresses. One said, "The only food here is what we get for ourselves. I'll prepare supper for you." Another brought an electrical socket with a light bulb; he twisted its wires onto two nails protruding from our concrete cell wall, and we had light. They gave us one tin can full of water, and another to use as a toilet during night hours. At 5 p.m. a guard came. He put us inside our cell, pulled the large heavy wooden door shut, and locked it with a dead bolt.

We had a two-room cell with concrete walls about 18 inches thick. The rooms were each about 6 by 8 feet, and were connected by an open doorway. The only window was an 18-by-24 inch opening above the locked door which served to ventilate both rooms. That night the temperature dropped to what felt like freezing. We lay on the floor in the darkness thinking about our families. Tim had four children, eight years old and under. Ned had three daughters, ages ten to 14. I had little Andrew. It could be a long time before we saw them again. The government could hold us up to 45 days without charges, before granting us a hearing. Our only friends were our fellow inmates, Muslim fundamentalists.

At 7 a.m. our door was opened. I wandered outside. Eight cell doors opened onto the central ward area. A low wall isolated one corner of the ward. Behind it on the floor was a gutter leading to an open toilet hole, and a full bucket of water for flushing.

Fellow prisoners continued friendly. They brought food and clothing. One of them brought a paint can. Inside it a heating coil rested on a layer of concrete. We hooked its two wires onto the wall nails, and it was a stove. It heated food and curbed the cold at night.

We learned the government accused us of fomenting sectarian sedition that endangered social stability, thereby circumventing possible accusations of its having violated the U.N. Declaration of Human Rights. I think our arrest was purely political. The government's heavy crackdown on Muslim Fundamentalists fostered rumors that it was becoming anti-Muslim. So it arrested some Westerners to balance the scales.

Prisoners frequently discussed religion. One day we shared our faith in Christ. We were not rejected for our beliefs. We began discussing them openly.

On day 10 I was called into the warden's office. There sat Dianne holding Andrew! I began crying and trembling.

I assured her that it wasn't because they were mistreating me. The prison staff were ordinary persons doing their jobs; it was the men at Secret Police headquarters who enjoyed making people suffer.

Thereafter our wives visited us once a week. They brought us books, writing materials, two new garbage cans (one for water, one for a toilet), our study Bibles. Dianne smuggled in an Arabic Bible for me. They staggered visits so that every other day one of our wives came, bringing us food enough for two days.

Our wives had their own troubles. For almost a month, two police cars were parked outside Dianne's apartment building 24 hours a day; whenever she left, they followed her. She was getting unnerving phone calls from the apartment's owners; they were trying to evict her.

All the trees in front of Tim's house were cut down to facilitate police surveillance. We learned the father of Asharof had committed him to a psychiatric ward.

Normally we four men got along well. Now, because of stress and our close confinement, we began getting on each other's nerves. We argued over petty things like personal hygiene habits. Ned became claustrophobic; he would shake, or hyperventilate, or cry uncontrollably. We gave him his own cell.

We smuggled out a letter to Ray, one of our team members. We wanted to know what was being done for our release. At length, he responded that Bob, our business manager in the States, was following instructions from the State Department. He was keeping the issue low profile, lest it embarrass the government holding us.

We were infuriated. Tim wrote, "Tell Bob that if this government is embarrassed on the international level, it will be glad to release us. I am still team leader. We want this incident full-blown in the media. Mount a letter-writing campaign. Get people to phone their representatives in government."

Ray relayed Bob's reply: "You are not in a position to make such a judgment. I am going to do it my way."

This discouraged us. How could this situation bring

glory to God? Nobody was doing the ministry God had called us to. Team members outside were occupied with efforts to secure our release. We felt this was wrong. We spent a week praying and two days fasting. We felt that, in the interests of God's kingdom, we should be released.

Our legal 45-day detainment passed. On day 50 we were told to get ready for a hearing at the court house. As an act of faith, we packed our bags for deportation.

The guards handcuffed 10 of us prisoners and packed us, kneeling or squatting, into a small covered pickup. They hauled us to the Court House. We waited inside the truck four hours. Then they returned us to prison; our names hadn't come up that day.

Next morning we went again. Guards placed us in a holding cell, still handcuffed. Other prisoners were brought, among them, Asharof! We clustered for an update.

"How are you doing?"

"When I arrived at the psychiatric ward, they tied me onto a bed frame. They wanted to give me a 'psychological test.' They tossed wild cats onto my bare chest. When I screamed, they said, 'See. He's crazy.' They left me tied down until now."

"How is your faith?"

"This has been very hard; but I am still trusting."

How our hearts reached out to him! The court would likely drop formal charges against him, and commit him indefinitely to a mental institution.

We began pacing the floor praying for our release. Something clicked inside me saying it had already been decided. Finally, they unhandcuffed four of us and took us to the judge. He, the prosecutor, and our defense attorney began conversing intensely in Arabic; we couldn't understand them.

The judge asked us in English, "Are you guilty, or not guilty?"

"Not guilty."

The judge argued in Arabic with our defense attorney. The hearing lasted about five minutes. Then guards took us back outside the Court House. They handcuffed us. The truck was waiting for us at the foot of the stone steps.

"Are they releasing us?" I asked a guard.

"No. They're holding you for another 45 days."

My world went black. Why was God refusing to answer our prayers? Where was he now?

We were returned to our prison ward. I went into the toilet cell to be alone. I stayed there for about 30 minutes, just crying my heart out. Doesn't God want to show that he is more powerful than the Muslims' God? Is my faith no better than theirs? Does it have any value? At that moment my belief system collapsed.

I felt that God at least owed me an explanation. I immersed myself in reading the Bible and prayer. At the end of three days, I had no answer; but I did find comfort in the book of Lamentations. The prophet Jeremiah also found himself in an unjust prison situation; he too thought God had abandoned him. This began reshaping my understanding of suffering as a part of the Christian experience.

The warden knew we were deeply disappointed. He called us into his office and bought us Cokes. I began spending more time with a sheik I had befriended; he had been in here for 15 years. He gave me daily lessons in Arabic; we used my Arabic Bible as text.

Bob in the States changed his opinion and began mounting a publicity campaign for our release. This encouraged us. But misunderstanding developed between Tim in prison and team members outside. Tim felt they were renouncing his authority; they seemed to keep doing things their way. In frustration, Tim resigned as team leader. The dispute so upset Bob, our business manager, that he too resigned. This left us no representative in the States. Things were a mess.

Tim slipped into deep depression; he felt everyone was against him. For days, he sat in the same spot reading his spy novels, speaking to no one. Finally, apologies were made in a letter. Ray got permission to visit prison. He and Tim talked, and eventually things came back together again.

Soon thereafter, one day the warden called us into his

office. As we entered, his deputy said, "Shhh. . ." The warden was on the phone. When he hung up he said, "I've been talking with the police station; I didn't want them to know that you were in the room. They are looking for your passports; we think they are going to release you." Both of them were so happy for us. They put on a cassette of Arabic music and began to dance; and suddenly we were dancing with them.

The next day the warden called us; police wanted the numbers of our credit cards. We assumed they wanted money to buy our air tickets. At 8 o'clock the next morning the warden called us again:

"They have scheduled a truck to come here and pick you up about 1 p.m."

This surely was it! We started telling everybody goodbye. We gave them all our things. When I returned my mattress to its owner, I learned he'd been sleeping on boards. We visited an Egyptian-American who'd been there for five years; we had led him to Christ. We gave him most of our books, and had prayer with him. My sheik friend asked for my Arabic Bible; I gave it to him.

On this, our 78th day, the truck came and hauled us to a holding cell at the airport. At flight time armed guards uncuffed us. They took us through the main section of the airport, our wives and other travellers watching. They boarded us onto the plane, gave us our passports, and left.

It remains for Ernie to share with us lessons he and his coworkers learned from their experience.

12

Lessons
from Prison

Persons called to serve God in hostile environ-
ments will gain insights from Ernie's reflection
on his particular experience.

Author: *What things were in place prior to your departure that proved very important?*

Ernie: First, having a business manager in the States.
The role of our business manager, Bob, was primarily secular. He gave our business a legitimate identity. He facilitated its function and development. He lived in Washington, D.C., where he could build bridges to key persons in
government. He had a lawyer friend who was familiar with
the workings of the State Department. He touched base
with human rights organizations. Traditionally, when missionaries encounter trouble with a foreign government,
their mission agency takes action on their behalf. But our
situation did not allow that. If our agency went public with
the issue, that action would expose and hazard our agency's
work internationally. That's why a knowledgeable secular
agent is so important.

When we were arrested, Bob contacted the State Department. He understood the importance of not identifing us as
evangelists or church planters in liaison with a foreign mission agency. This would prompt State Department officials
to say, "Why are they in a country which doesn't allow missionaries? They got what they deserved." Bob also interceded

on our behalf with our congressional representatives.

Secondly, having a large network of people to pray for us and to participate in a letter-writing campaign. Bob mounted this campaign. The network grew to include people on the prayer mailing lists of team members; pastors in all churches of our denominations (they activated their parishioners); mailing lists of other mission agencies who work among Muslims; base offices of these agencies in foreign countries (their constituents lodged complaints with our host country's U. S. embassies); and the mailing lists of human rights organizations. Because of the flood of mail, the State Department began to act for us, and top government people in our host country began seeing that our detainment was angering people all over the world.

A third thing that proved very important was our computer equipped with electronic mail (e-mail). Messages were confidential because they were scrambled, or "encrypted." Bob's computer in the States has the program for unscrambling them. Our wives could tell Bob exactly what had happened to us on any given day. Our team leader could ask Bob a question in the morning, and receive his answer that afternoon.

Author: *How did your experience change your feelings about the methodology of allowing converts to remain within their Muslim culture?*

Ernie: It served to reinforce them. This method is still experimental, but we feel it was the best approach for our situation. It seems to be the most natural way to plant low profile house churches with national leadership. There is the view that the missionary's adoption of Muslim customs may bring him into more severe persecution when his purposes of witnessing for Christ are disclosed. We found the contrary to be true. Our consistent efforts to identify with their culture enhanced their respect for us. Everybody who knew us well, knew we were followers of Christ.

By the time we were arrested, bonding was such that all who knew us were baffled and shocked that the government would do such a thing.

Author: *Does not this strategy invite the syncretism of biblical truth with the beliefs of Islam?*

Ernie: In our case syncretism was not an issue because while the people were Muslim culturally, the vast majority was not Muslim theologically. We simply assumed their "theological slate" was uncluttered, and began teaching the Bible. When they made a commitment to Christ, they committed themselves to what we had taught them. They didn't come back to us saying, "But the Koran says otherwise." The average Muslim doesn't know what the Koran says. I cannot say whether this would hold equally true for countries with a stronger theological base in Islam.

Author: *In retrospect, what do you see should have been done differently?*

Ernie: First, we should have developed stronger bonds with the U.S. Embassy. We should have gone to embassy parties, just to hobnob with people. We should have joined the American Chamber of Commerce there. Some of our team members should have been occupied full-time in developing the business. Such efforts would have proved helpful later on.

Second, Dianne and I should have better educated our churches and our network of supporters about what precisely we were doing. They needed to understand our strategy, and the reasons for it. Some of them were really baffled when they learned we were adopting Muslim customs. Others could not understand why they could not refer to us as "missionaries" when they wrote their government representatives on our behalf. When we were arrested, it fell to Bob and our parents to educate pastors and church people about what we were doing. Only then would these persons lend their support to work for our release. I've learned that people do understand the concept when we explain it to them.

There is some risk that such information could fall into the wrong hands and be used against us, but it's worth the risk. We asked people not to circulate our letters, not to post them for general reading. There is no foolproof way of keeping such information from the wrong people.

Third, one must be extremely cautious about what information is given to the press. Such information should be released through one designated spokesperson. We are free agents, and have no inherent obligation to the press. When our best interests are served, we have the right to withhold information.

Fourth, the chances are maybe one in a hundred that contingency plans will be used; but they should be in place before a crisis arises. What authority does a team leader retain if he is imprisoned? Who then takes responsibility for implementing the team leader's wishes? In case the team leader is removed from the picture, who replaces him? In the chain-of-command, how does the business manager function in relationship to the team leader?

Dianne and I would also want a plan in place in the States for mounting a letter-writing campaign. If she phones my parents one evening that I have been imprisoned, next morning a plan would be put into action.

Author: *Why not form teams of persons with compatible temperaments and complementary gifts prior to departure for the field?*

Ernie: In most cases, entry of a group at one time gives the event too high a profile. This could provoke the government's intervention or denial of entry. Ours was the more traditional approach. The team leader, already familiar with the situation on the field, decides who will and will not be invited to join his team. He receives a file for each candidate with the results of psychological tests, and recommendations about where and how this couple might best fit into a team. In our case, each couple signed up for a two-year term, at the end of which the team leader and the couple, together, decided about the future.

A team where all members have compatible temperaments will not likely be the most effective team. Its creativity would be limited, and its viewpoint very narrowly focused. It is much more important that team members have skills in conflict resolution.

Then the issue is not "How do we avoid conflict?", but "How are we going to resolve it?" Sometimes disagreements on our team sparked heated discussions, but we worked through our differences. This probably helps explain why 95 percent of the teams under our agency do not have severe interpersonal problems.

Author: *What could have been done to enhance the effectiveness of the team?*
Ernie: Personally I feel that if we had had more individual freedom and flexibility, there could have been more success. All learning, strategy, and methodology came from the level of the team leader down. If your vision and motivation are borrowed from your team leader, the ministry is limited to the vision and ability of the leader. A blind follower cannot deal with obvious mistakes. And if one person makes a mistake, all must take responsibility for it because all are copies of one another.

Most teams are more flexible than ours. They are small: two or three couples. Often couples are allowed to work independently. They read books in their field, explore strategies, and decide for themselves what is useful and what is not. Teams have a group meeting once or twice a week to make sure they are still on target towards a common goal. In my view, this flexibility should increase overall team effectiveness, and also would reduce the likelihood of ongoing relational conflicts.

Author: *How did relational bridges built to nationals help you?*
Ernie: One time I took Andrew to visit the owner of a small shoe store; I had met him on my language-learning circuit. He insisted on giving my son a pair of shoes. He was a Muslim fundamentalist. He invited me to the birthday party of his son. Fundamentalists requested that I come to the mosque two nights a week to teach their children English, which I was planning to do. Because of friendly relations we had built, we were sharing our faith openly. And no one, even the fundamentalists, saw us as a

threat to Islam.

Muslim neighbors in the apartment across the hall from us had been living in the building for about 20 years. After my arrest, they gave Dianne great support. The wives of my three prison mates were evicted from their homes. When pressure was building on our landlord to evict Dianne, our Muslim neighbors went to him and said, "These people have been through enough. If you evict them, you evict us also." They came to Dianne and said, "If they kick you and your son out, you are just moving across the hall with us. If he insists that you leave our place, he'll have to kick us out too." When it seemed Diane's eviction was imminent, they came and helped her pack her things.

Author: *What qualities of your wife emerged as very important?*

Ernie: Courage to carry on with life under very difficult circumstances. Flexibility to adapt to situations that were changing on a daily basis. A strong, steady faith in God. Stamina under stress is probably one of the most important things. Her round-the-clock surveillance by government authorities was very stressful. The apartment owner was calling her during nights screaming into the phone that she should get out. Her hot water was cut off. When she came to visit me, she told me these things, but she never broke down and cried in my presence. She saved that for when she was at home.

Author: *What lessons did you learn regarding husband-wife relationships?*

Ernie: A deep, commonly shared sense of calling is paramount. That basic commitment means we will stick together, no matter what. My internment was harder on Dianne than it was on me. For four days she didn't know where I was. She had to continue providing a home for our son, his food, his nap time, his birthday party. Sometimes she couldn't bathe for days; or she couldn't sleep for more than three hours at a time. I was bathing every day, and sleeping well every night.

A wife shouldn't feel guilty about leaving the country for a break from the stress. But she must have persons who can offer her emotional support. Fortunately, Dianne had close relatives in a nearby country. At first she said, "I feel guilty taking a vacation while you are here in prison." I said, "My basic needs are being met. I can deal with the separation. Do what is needful for you. Go get a break."

About three weeks into our detainment, Tim and his wife agreed that she should return with their four small children to the States. She planned to visit him once every six months. A good church friend of Ned and his wife came to visit and to offer support. When he returned, he took their three daughters back with him so the girls could resume their schooling.

Men and women view enduring hardship differently. A man is more inclined to say, "This is part of what it is to follow Christ, of embracing the cross." The wife says, "But what about your family? Don't you care about us?" A couple should work at processing this issue prior to a crisis.

Even after my release, the experience affected us differently. When we had relocated outside the country, I wanted to celebrate my freedom from confinement. I wanted to be out at night. I wanted to run all over the place. My wife had been giving so much of herself to me, and to Andrew, and to the other wives, she just wanted to crash and sleep and see no one.

Presently, I find talking about the experience cathartic. For her, it revives memories she is trying to put to rest.

On a practical level, both husband and wife should have credit cards. They should have a joint bank account. Should he be incarcerated, she must have access to funds.

Author: *Much of the credit for the accomplishments of the global missionary enterprise over the past two centuries must go to single missionary women. In your account, no single women are mentioned. Why?*

Ernie: History witnesses to the remarkable achievements of single missionary women, even in hostile settings. However, in a Muslim culture, special conditions prevail.

Some Muslim countries do not allow the entry of foreign single women. Our country does; but the common conception is that Western women are loose and easily available. Muslim women wear Western-style dresses until they are married; this symbolizes their availability. Upon marriage, they adopt traditional clothing which covers most exposed parts of the body. Their husband may have other wives.

A Western single missionary woman relocating into a Muslim setting would have to deal with the advances of Muslim men. She could dress like a Muslim married woman. But then Muslim women would say, "Why is she like this? What is wrong with her?" Female singleness is unnatural where Islam is strong. If a single missionary woman surmounted these challenges, she could teach missionary children, share her faith with Muslim women, or fill a role in the field of medicine.

Author: *What is the status of the believers your team left behind?*

Ernie: Three of the women continue to meet regularly; one of them has led her brother to Christ. One of the men has begun meeting with a group of believers again. The last word we heard, Asharof had remained tied to the bed so long that he was paralyzed from the waist down, and his health was deteriorating.

Author: *What important thing did your experience teach you regarding the Christian faith?*

Ernie: The role of suffering. Before we left the States, Dianne and I had talked about suffering. We knew it was possible; but we never expected it to hurt. Now we know it does. North America's affluent society infers that human beings do not need to suffer. Our experience turned that thinking completely around.

When we were sentenced to another 45 days in prison, I was at the lowest point in my life. My first reaction was that it makes absolutely no sense. Then I felt that if it did make sense, God at least owed me an explanation. Later, I came to see that neither of these views is biblical.

Sometimes God chooses to be glorified through deliverance. Sometimes he chooses to be glorified through suffering, and through our praise in the midst of suffering. Of the heroes of faith listed in Hebrews chapter 11, some were delivered, some were not. God did not provide those who were not delivered with an explanation.

I came across something written by Jim Elliot, who was martyred by the Auca Indians. In Psalm 100, verses three and four, we read that the Lord is God, that we are his sheep, and that we are to enter his courts with thanksgiving and praise. Jim asks, "Why are the sheep ever brought into the temple of God? The only reason is to be sacrificed." Maybe God saw me as one of those sheep. I could not control my situation. I could not leave. It was not up to me to understand why. It was up to me to offer God thanksgiving and praise. That was very hard.

Maybe the most effective thing God can use to bring Muslims to Christ is their observing the suffering of believers. Greg Livingstone wrote recently, "Is there any breakthrough on earth which was not preceded by years of suffering?"[1]

Maybe a lot more of us will need to go to jail.

---

1. Greg Livingstone, "Needed: Christians Who Will Die; the Challenge of Muslim Evangelism," *Prism*, February, 1994, p. 12.

13

Revolution

We who have grown up in the U.S. or Canada are fortunate. We are imbued with great historic Christian traditions. Our governments have granted us freedom of speech, of religion, and of the pursuit of happiness. They provide us with a stable social environment. This has enabled the vast majority of us to grow; to grow numerically; to grow in material wealth; to grow in personal fulfillment; and to live healthier, longer lives. For Christians, a free, competitive market has produced multiple resources which presumably foster spiritual growth.

My family and I were with Africans through two periods of violent political upheaval. Those experiences taught me that historic tradition, ordered society, and a free competitive market in themselves do not produce heroes of faith.

Zaire, with a population of 40 million, is as large as the United States east of the Mississippi River. Belgium developed in Zaire (then the Belgian Congo) a stable and progressive society. Expanding agricultural production and minimum wage laws gradually raised Zairians' standard of living. They were beginning to enjoy material benefits with which I was familiar. Stores were full of merchandise. Roads were well-maintained. A postal system worked smoothly. For my first nine years there as a missionary, I felt comfortable and secure. I rejoiced that Zairians, too, lived in an environment of freedom and security where their faith could grow.

But Belgium never taught the Zairians self-government. The winds of nationalism sweeping Africa compelled Belgium to grant Zaire political independence on June 30,

1960. In a few days, Belgians began to panic and flee by the thousands. The fledgling nation's army demanded a raise in salary; failing this, soldiers at a key military base overthrew their commanders. Mutiny spread rapidly to points across the country. Bands of military personnel settled grievances against whites by shooting, beating, terrorizing, vandalizing, and raping. Security evaporated. Tribal peoples who harbored ancient grievances seized the moment to even scores. They raided adjacent villages of their perceived adversaries. This ignited tribal warfare.

We missionaries, too, were potential victims of ravaging soldiers and angry tribespeople. Wild rumors fed our fears. A radio network linked our eight stations where missionaries lived; we kept in touch with each other. Anarchy advanced towards us from the east.

Our best escape would be westward. Such escape depended upon crossing a river by ferry. This pressed us to a common decision: we would risk driving the roads to relocate across the river, before the ferry fell into unfriendly hands. We would relocate at our western station, Kandala, which also was on a direct route leading 200 miles south to the border of Angola.

We were three missionary couples at our station. Missionary colleague Glenn and I were reluctant to comply with the decision. We loathed abandoning our national Christians. I was a radio ham; my contacts with other hams could keep us informed of trends.

Early that afternoon, a caravan of vehicles heavily loaded with missionaries and baggage, travelling west, stopped for us to join them. Glenn and I declined. We sent our wives and children on ahead, and remained alone.

Towards evening Glenn and I called a meeting of our local believers. Tearfully, we explained our dilemma. We offered to stay and share their destiny. A deep forested ravine bordered the station. If mutinying troops looking for whites should arrive, Glenn and I could hide in the ravine. Believers listened to our offer, but gave no opinion.

Belgian operators at an airport control tower 165 miles east of us had promised help in an emergency. That evening I learned by radio that it had fallen to mutinying troops. Increasingly, ham signals on my radio dial were falling silent. I heard a distress call from a group of besieged Europeans expecting to be massacred within the hour.

The next morning the local church pastor came. He said that our idea to hide in the forest was not helpful to the church people. Glenn and I did not know which berries, leaves, and roots were edible, and which were poison. For us to survive, believers would have to bring us food. If lawless soldiers arrived, believers would be beaten into disclosing our whereabouts. Our presence hazarded their safety. Reluctantly, Glenn and I gave the pastor all of the station keys, said goodbye, and drove west to Kandala.

Some 30 refugee missionaries and children were there. By radio we followed the disintegration of law and order. Spreading anarchy threatened to encircle us. We prayed. We dialogued. We were wrenched by indecision. Eventually it became clear that here, too, our presence as whites jeopardized the safety of the church which was concerned with protecting us. We agreed that our best course was to proceed south, casting ourselves upon God's mercy to see us through a roadblock at a military post 200 miles distant, and to relocate across the border into Angola.

Fellow missionary Pete and I loaded our wives, baggage, and seven children into a Chevy van. We left Kandala about 3 p.m. Some 15 miles out, a front spring pin sheared, forcing us to return. We arrived back at Kandala at about sundown. All the missionaries had left; we were in effect stranded.

Pete had left his VW bug here, because it was stalling from apparent ignition problems. Now he decided he would have to take it after all. The local national church owned a pickup. We asked the pastor if somehow they could help us catch up with the other missionaries. He called a meeting of the church council. They agreed that their chauffeur, Andrew, could drive their truck and provide us transportation until we found the other missionaries. We loaded tools and a barrel of gas into the pickup. We knew that rampaging soldiers were raping white women. About 8 p.m. Andrew,

our three older boys and I climbed into the pickup. We
went first. Pete, our wives, three daughters and small son,
all in the VW bug, followed us.

Progress was slow. The bug stalled. Then it got stuck in
the sand. It stalled again. Andrew proved a better me-
chanic than either Pete or I. Through the night, cars from
our rear streaked past, the red glow of their tail lights disappearing into the darkness ahead of us.

I mentally prepared for the military roadblock. Soldiers
wanted higher wages. I put $100 in my right coat pocket.
When the roadblock soldier stopped us, I would roll down
the window and give it to him. l would tell him that we
were missionaries who had no affair against them. I would
ask for permission to pass. If he insisted on seeing white
man's blood, I would volunteer the little finger on my left
hand. If this did not satisfy him, I hoped whatever happened would take place behind some structure so that my
wife and children would not witness it. Having made this
plan, I was at peace.

Our headlights caught a soldier. I checked my watch:
2:15 a.m. He extended his bayonetted rifle across the road.
We stopped. I rolled down the window. Before I could start
my speech, he was asking Andrew questions. Andrew answered. The tone was friendly. The soldier knew Andrew
from previous trips the pickup had made through that
area. Praise the Lord for Andrew!

"Stop at military headquarters in the center of town and
get a permit to leave," the soldier ordered. We drove the few
miles into the center of town. We saw no light anywhere.
Two seconds of indecision, and I said to Andrew, "Give it the
gun!" He did. I checked in the rearview mirror; the VW was
following us. A few miles south of town we stopped, had
prayers of thanksgiving, refueled, and continued. At 5 a.m.
we reached the border. Soldiers lounged around a bonfire.
Apparently they were not yet affected by the mutiny. I went
and engaged them in light conversation. At 7 a.m. they
roused their commanding officer. He completed our documents, and we crossed the frontier. A few miles further, at
a rushing stream, we found the caravan of missionaries who

had camped the night there, waiting for us.

Within days we missionaries were air-evacuated to Canada and the U.S. Behind us, our Zairian friends slipped into a fearsome valley of violence, bloodshed, destruction, and death. I drop the curtain on Act One.

Two years later my family and I returned. We lived in Kananga, a city of 100,000. By now corruption had infiltrated all levels of government. Political dissenters were chased into exile.

Civil servants' pay was poor. School graduates found no employment. Roads fell into disrepair. Crime was mounting. Disenchantment was widespread.

Zairian political exiles found training in China. They gained the support of China for an armed insurrection against the Zairian government. The effort was launched in January of 1964. A government post in the province west of us was burned to the ground, its personnel killed. Disorders there spread rapidly throughout that province, and then were uneasily contained at its borders.

Meanwhile, insurgents launched invasions from across Zaire's eastern frontier. Disenchanted youth rushed to join them. The movement spread like wildfire. By August two-thirds of the country had fallen to rebel forces. In September, national headquarters of "The People's Republic" was set up in the major northeastern city of Kisanganyi. The insurgents' policy was to raze everything to the ground. Reportedly, their foreign friends would enable total reconstruction. Rebels cowered people into submission by publicly executing a notable; by burying a person alive up to his neck; or by other forms of calculated torture. Often they targeted pastors and leading Christians.

The rumor was widespread that rebel forces had witchcraft medicine that turned soldiers' bullets into water. Retreating government forces reportedly said, "We shoot and shoot, but they just keep on coming."

During July we listened to daily radio reports and followed the ominous approach of rebel forces. Missionary pilot Burley Law airlifted women and children from a large Methodist mission station 150 miles north of us. Rebel troops arrived, and took the five men missionaries captive. Burley landed to assist them. When he refused to give rebels the keys to his plane, he was shot in the stomach, and died on the operating table.

Advancing rebel forces arrived at Lusambo, the last large city to our north. They jammed people into thatch-roofed houses, locked the doors, and ignited the roofs. They executed my good friend, national pastor John Ishaku, by machine gun, in full view of his wife and five small children. The city of Lusambo fell.

Our city swelled with refugees. They brought shocking stories of suffering. Military trucks hauling flag-draped caskets passed by our front door on their way to the Catholic church. Only our city stood in the way of insurgents linking with their comrades already holding the province west of us; this would bisect the country. Then rebels transmitted a radio message that they would arrive at our city on August 15.

A rumor spread that government soldiers were going to kill the pro-rebel element of our city's population; thus they could better withstand the rebel attack. The city became an armed camp. Angry women clad only in loin cloths demonstrated in the streets. Banging metal kitchen pots in rhythm, they refused their husbands food or bed, until they went and fought the rebels. All of us faced increasingly imminent violence and possible death.

How do such events affect a person long rooted in political and material security? I confess that fear pummeled and buffeted me. The daily bombardment of rumors, the climate of uncontrolled disorder and terror, the raw, calculated infliction of human suffering, the slow starvation of people hidden in forests trying to escape it all. I could find nothing that had prepared me for this.

Jesus taught that when we suffer for righteousness sake, we are to rejoice (literally, leap for joy), right? I had neither the ability nor inclination to rejoice. American Christians read that "all who live godly in Christ Jesus shall suffer persecution" (2 Tim. 3:12) and wonder when they'll be given such an opportunity. Now I had one, and didn't want it. I should have been praying for Zairians in rebel-controlled areas whom I knew were suffering and dying. Instead, I found my mind increasingly anxious about the welfare of my wife, my children, and myself.

I remembered my Bible school days, when I'd thought it would be a joy to someday lay my head onto the chopping block for Jesus. I remember other occasions in Congo where I'd faced possible death calmly: by a nervous, angry soldier with a loaded rifle; by a madman who later strangled a woman. Stress seems to peak while one waits for the inevitable moment of encounter. During the long night hours of travelling with Andrew towards that military roadblock, I had been at peace. Now, waiting for the moment of encounter was quite different. Stress ominously stripped back layer after layer of my faith until it exposed the center core of self-preservation. As Eliphaz told Job long ago, "Think how you have instructed many, how you have strengthened feeble hands. Your words have supported those who stumbled; you have strengthened faltering knees. But now trouble comes to you, and you are discouraged; it strikes you, and you are dismayed" (Job 4:3-5).

An old Zairian evangelist, long my friend, was now in the local hospital with a terminal heart condition. I visited him to offer encouragement. Our conversation turned to the rebels' threat to our city.

"Isn't God all powerful any more?" he asked.

"Yes, he is."

"Isn't God able to turn back these rebels?"

"Well, yes he is."

"I'm going to pray to God that he do something powerful like he did in the olden days."

One morning I opened the office windows and tried focusing my attention to waiting business on my desk. A cough at the window distracted me. Standing outside was an old Christian, a church elder, leaning on his walking staff. He had undergone two operations for chest cancer, and was again beginning to suffer pain. His home was about two miles distant, on the edge of the city.

"Good morning, Speaker," he respectfully greeted me.

"Good morning, Tshimanga. Won't you come in?"

He seated himself in my office.

"Speaker, I've come to pray with you," he said. "I know these are hard days for you; I want to ask God to strengthen your heart."

We knelt by our chairs. For perhaps five minutes he poured out his heart to God on our behalf—that we would continue to give ourselves to the work; that our hearts be filled with courage; that God would protect us in any eventuality. Then he rose, shook hands, picked up his walking staff. With the slow measured steps of a man in pain, he turned and left.

Only later that day the impact of what had happened struck me. That man had submitted himself to at least four hours of pain for the few minutes he spent with me. I could see him walking a few yards, then leaning against a fence post to rest, then walking again. Why hadn't I offered to drive him home? My preoccupation with the personal safety of my family and myself made me calloused and insensitive to the needs of a human being in pain.

I couldn't afford to share my fears with my Zairian co-workers; I had been sent to Zaire to teach them how to trust the Lord, you know. But I felt I had to know if they were experiencing the inner turmoil I was. And so I asked a few guarded questions.

John Kamba, a Zairian writer working with me, said, "Yes, these are difficult days. But we have had hard days before, and God took care of us. After a time, these affairs will pass too."

I asked Pastor Matthew Kazadi. He replied, "Our rulers are scrapping with each other for power. We can't trouble ourselves with their palavers. We've got too much work to do."

Pastor Thomas Kabangu, with a beaming smile, said, "Sure, we can flee for our lives. We've done it before. But when Jesus comes back, it's best that he find us with our hands in the work. Let's not be afraid. Let's carry on. A few weeks ago I baptized 108 new believers. I'm pastor of six different areas. I've got 40,000 francs in our church treasury. We've placed evangelist-teachers in villages and are paying them regularly."

What had happened to all of my self-assumed maturity? These men were no longer my understudies. They had withstood a few years of deprivation and suffering. Now, they were my mentors. I found comfort in their shadows.

On the morning of August 9, I drove a refugee missionary family to the airport so they could relocate to a more stable environment. We passed three large military trucks along the roadside. They were packed with soldiers, camouflaged helmets in place, shoulder-hung bandoliers of cartridges criss-crossing their chests, rifles in hand. Drivers were checking tire pressure, about to embark on the journey north to engage with rebel forces approaching the city to meet tomorrow's deadline.

I returned to the city. Businesses were closed. The streets were empty. Foxholes were dug. Barbed wire was unrolled. People were at home, waiting. Fear was palpable.

That night we half-slept, with ears perked for the sounds of battle.

Next morning news arrived: when the convoy of troops rounded a sharp bend in the road, suddenly they were confronted by 12 truckloads of advancing rebels. Such timing allowed no thoughts of retreat. The soldiers opened fire, decimating the rebels, and disabling 11 trucks. Stragglers fled in the 12th one. The soldiers, sustaining few losses, pursued them.

I returned to the old evangelist in the hospital.

"Tshisungu," I said, "God answered your prayers. He did something mighty, like in the olden days."

Must today's cross-cultural missionaries anticipate such experiences? Unfortunately, yes. Within the past 18 months, eight missionaries have been kidnapped. Liberia lies devastated from a three-way civil war that is stalemated; over a million refugees from Rwanda seek haven in Zaire. Drug trafficking, political corruption, and crushing poverty destabilize some countries in Latin America.

Global instability will increase.[1] Certain factors make this trend inevitable: the resurgence of ethnic violence; the decrease in arable land due to slash-and-burn techniques;

the depletion of other scarce natural resources; the growing chasm between the rich and poor; population growth; (according to the Academy of Science, 95 percent of population increase will be in the poorest regions of the world); and the ongoing transfer of government expenditures away from education and health, to administrative costs (salaries for bureaucrats, and increased military expenditures to keep restive populations under control).[2]

In the light of these facts, what can you, a cross-cultural missionary candidate or missionary, do to prepare yourself for a climate of political instability? You can familiarize yourself with the growing body of literature on the subject. Study the social, economic, and political dynamics of your host culture. Study the history of your host country. Is its present social climate pre-revolutionary, in revolution, or post-revolutionary? Draw upon the experiences of persons who have lived through political upheaval. Finally, what is the policy of your mission board regarding payment of ransom for kidnapped missionaries? Is its position part of a published policy statement? Are you in agreement with the position?

Percentage-wise, very few missionaries are killed or injured because of political instability. But the work of an ever increasing number is affected by it. The nature of our contemporary world behooves us to be prepared.

---

1. Robert D. Kaplan, "The Coming Anarchy," *Atlantic Monthly*, February, 1994, p. 44.

2. From 1972 to 1985, percentage of expenditures for education in Zaire declined from 15.2 to .8; those for health from 2.3 to 1.8; and those for public administration have increased from 56.1 to 86.2. In the same time frame, and categories, percentage of expenditures in Mexico have been from 16.4 to 12.4; 5.1 to 1.5; and from 15.2 to 44.4. The trend is typical of most Two-Thirds World countries. Charles K. Wilber and Kenneth P. Jameson, *The Political Economy of Development and Underdevelopment* (New York: McGraw-Hill, 1973), p. 589.

14

"We're Coming for a Visit!"

Two couples, Fred and Francis, and Art and Alice, members of Bethel Community Church, decide to visit Margaret, the missionary their church supports in Africa. Each feels their visit must have a mission.

Fred, a farmer, wonders why Africans remain forever so poor. "Everything we have in this country came from the soil," he says. "Those people have soil. What stands in the way of their growing crops and improving their condition like we do?" Fred plans to take a soil-testing kit to determine what the soil needs to make it produce.

Art is a car salesman. He believes that a nation's commercial growth hinges upon improving transportation. He sees Africa as a great untapped market for motorbikes.

In early June Francis writes to Margaret on the field, informing her of their pending visit.

"Please don't go to any trouble for us," she says. "We only plan to stay for about two weeks. We just want to get a first-hand look at what you're doing so we can encourage the people here at Bethel Church to strengthen their support. We would like to come in early August."

In mid-July the letter reached Margaret on her rural mission station. She called a meeting with her four missionary colleagues: a couple in their mid-thirties, and a couple in their mid-fifties. She read Francis' letter to them. There was an awkward silence.

"Well, it's too late for us to answer them," senior missionary Russ thought aloud. "Our reply wouldn't reach them before they leave."

"We could radio a message to Bill at Kampoto to send Francis a telegram," Dale the younger missionary suggested.

"What are we going to tell her?" asked Russ's wife Elaine.

Again there was silence.

"We can hardly discourage them from coming," Margaret replied. "Squelching their enthusiasm would have a negative impact upon the church's missionary support."

"That's true," Russ replied. "We need to allow them to come."

"But we don't have enough canned goods in stock to feed them for two weeks," Elaine said.

"Well, that means a shopping trip to Kampoto: a day to go, a day to shop, and a day to come home," Dale replied. "Who's taking three days out of their schedule?"

Nobody volunteered.

"Then there are matters of budget," Russ continued. "With canned goods double the price they are in the States, who pays for the food? And with gas at $12 dollars a gallon, who pays for the travel costs?"

"How many trips to Kampoto are we talking about?" Margaret asked.

"Is the van large enough to haul them and our food purchases on the same trip?" Russ queried.

"With the amount of baggage folks from the States normally bring with them, no way," Dale replied.

"Then that means two trips to Kampoto."

"That's more than I can pay for," Margaret concluded.

"We wouldn't expect you to cover such costs," Russ explained. "Maybe we can take it from our contingency funds."

"Will the home board approve of our using those funds that way?" Dale asked. "I mean, the board had no part in planning the trip."

"Good point," Russ replied. "Especially when there is a 10 percent shortfall in giving to missions this year. We'll just have to pass the burden on to the board this time; maybe that will prompt it to draw up guidelines for handling situations like this."

On August 10 Margaret with an African chauffeur met the visiting party at Kampoto airport.

The bouncy, dusty trip home gave rise to some questions.

"You say it's five hours to your mission station? I thought you would just pick us up at the airport like we do at home."

"Did you choose this road because you want to show us what a bad road is like? Or are they all like this?"

"There's no room for passing. What happens if we meet somebody at the top of this hill?"

"Any place along the way for a rest stop and a cold drink?"

Just over two hours out, in the midst of tall savannah grass, Mildred told the chauffeur to pull over. "Rest stop," she announced. "Men to the left. Women to the right." The guests exchanged glances, hesitated, then began disappearing into the high grass.

At the mission station the guests settled in quickly. Margaret assigned them Kahnu as a guide. Kahnu had worked for the missionaries many years, was a pastor, and spoke English. Art observed that most Africans had bikes. But their bikes were in poor condition because repair parts were either unavailable, or too costly. Few Africans had incomes that allowed them to buy anything more than food and clothing for their families. Motorbikes would facilitate commerce. But neither motorbikes nor spare parts were manufactured within the country; they would have to be imported, and the government would tax a 100 percent custom fee on them.

Marketing motorbikes would require a much higher level of income, a banking system where buyers could invest savings, a marketing system for motorbikes, the availability of affordable spare parts, and mechanics to install them. It appeared this would take aeons of time.

Fred discovered that the soil was light, sandy, and sour. It would need compost and mulch to give it body, and lime for fertilizer. He found outcroppings of limestone which, if crushed and scattered on the soil, would sweeten it. Who would supply capital to build a fertilizer plant? Who would supply capital to purchase trucks for transporting fertilizer?

Who would keep the trucks in good repair? Who would assure a reliable supply of affordable spare parts? Would North Americans with sufficient capital invest in costly enterprises in countries ruled by greedy dictators and threatened by political coups?

At the end of the two-week visit, Fred and Art felt disillusioned. But Art was determined to make at least a small contribution.

"Kahnu," he said, "you have been our mouth, eyes, and ears. What can I do to help you?"

"I am a pastor," Kahnu replied. "I oversee 14 parishes. To make one trip to visit them all, I must walk on foot 85 miles. It would make my work much easier if I had a motorbike."

"I'll see that you get one," Art promised.

Upon returning home, Francis wanted to give a report to their congregation. She was allowed either 10 minutes during a Sunday morning worship service, or a separate Sunday evening. She took a Sunday evening. As normal, the attendance was low. An offering for missions was taken. People, feeling that they had fulfilled their obligation to Fred, Francis, Art, and Alice, filed the trip away in their memories.

Art bought a motorbike, and contacted the home office of the mission board for information on how to ship it. There was a delay in its response. Then the board informed him that there were 24 pastors like Kahnu who supervised large areas. They had already heard that Kahnu was receiving a motorbike. They said it was unfair. Why should Kahnu be set apart for such privilege? If he was given a motorbike, why should they not all receive motorbikes? The board asked Art not to proceed with his plan.

Art was bitter because he could not fulfill his promise. Margaret informed Kahnu that he would not be receiving a motorbike. When Kahnu shared the news with the pastors, they agreed, "It is always the mission board that stands in the way when people in America want to give us things."

The above story is not meant to discourage visits to a mission field. Missionaries want visits by people from the home church. The story is designed to show the confusion, misunderstanding, and disappointment which sometimes issue from visits that are not carefully planned. What should have been done to assure a positive outcome?

After Fred, Francis, Art, and Alice agreed that they wanted to visit Margaret, they should not have unilaterally decided that the trip would happen, when they would arrive, how long they would stay, and what they would do while on the field. Rather, they should have submitted their proposal to the church council. To advise them wisely, the council would contact the mission board and ask questions such as the following:

1. Is such a trip advisable?
2. If so, when should it occur?
3. What should be its time frame?
4. What are its approximate costs?
5. How are such costs normally covered?
6. Are there supplies or baggage of other missionaries the visitors could take with them?
7. Are there particular services these persons could render during their visit?

If the board deems the trip as useful, the church council would recommend to the people of the congregation that they send the two couples as their representatives to visit their missionary, undergirding them with its support of prayer and finances. If the congregation adopts the recommendation, plans should be made for an official farewell service to give the two couples a sense of mission and accountability. Meanwhile, the couples would meet with a representative of the home board for well-planned orientation so that they know what to expect and what not to expect; what is appropriate, and what is not appropriate.

Because the congregation has taken ownership of the planned visit, it will expect a report when its delegation returns. At that time, it could be invited to rethink its budget obligations to missions in the light of the delegation's updated information.

The following chapter deals with other ways to strengthen bonding between missionaries and the home church.

15

The Home Church

A standard link between the missionary and the home church is a periodic newsletter. The time you invest in preparing your newsletter reflects the value you attach to its readers. Following are 10 tips to help assure that the newsletters you mail are, in fact, read.

1. An Attractive Format

How can you make your stationery distinctive? Stamp it with a personal logo in colored ink? Create a caption? (A Message from Millers; Petersons' Pilgrimage; Columbian Clarion, Evans' Epistle, etc.)

We served in Africa. Before we left, I had an artist prepare two drawings. The first was a two-inch border for printing in colored ink at the top of stationery to be used as page one of our newsletters. At the top of the border were printed the words: pointing to men the Jesus way. The typeface leaned to the right, suggesting forward movement. Beneath it were silhouettes of Africans, all walking to the right on a green line representing a road. The second drawing showed half a palm tree, its half-trunk extending completely down the left side of the page; its fronds arching to the right across the top edge of the page. I printed a thousand sheets of each design, and left them with the person here in the U.S. who was in charge of duplicating and mailing our newsletters.

You may want to use pastel-colored paper instead of

white. Have ample margins on all four sides of the printed matter. Leave ample white space, perhaps by making shorter paragraphs, or by double spacing between paragraphs.

2. Interesting Content

You may find it helpful to collect potential resource material for your next newsletter in a file folder. When the time comes to write your letter, prepare an outline of your material to give it order and progression. A thumb rule for good writing is: make it clear, concise, and graphic. The most important part of a newsletter is its opening paragraph. Try to make it short and catchy. Narrate an experience. Be honest and realistic. Use a Scripture verse.

Occasionally include a picture. Typewriter keys include #, %, &, *, +, !, +, =. Use them to make boxes, column dividers, decorative symbols, and borders. Use boldface, italics, and underlining for highlighting. Unless something earth-shaking has happened, don't make your letter too long; one and one-half pages is a reader-friendly length.

3. Your mailing address

It should be complete, and clearly visible, either as a heading at the top of your letter, or at its end.

4. Clearly identify the author

There seems to be a spreading plague among newsletter writers to avoid the personal pronoun "I." If I read the name "Don" in the text, I automatically assume the author is his wife Mary. Until suddenly, without warning, I come to the word "Mary." Now who is talking to me? The author becomes some disembodied third entity nobody knows.

5. Sign the letter

At the end should be the personal signature of the author(s). If you have possession of all copies of your newsletter, sign each one, preferably using a different colored ink. If someone in the homeland duplicates your letter, your signature will be a photocopy of the original.

6. Decide upon the distribution point

Will you mail all the copies from where you serve on the field, or will someone in the homeland photocopy the letter and mail it? Often the deciding factor is economy. If mailing costs where you serve are comparable with those at home, you have an advantage; people always enjoy receiving a letter with exotic postage stamps from overseas.

7. Mail your letter in a distinguishable envelope

Your addressee, upon receiving the letter, must immediately distinguish it from junk mail. We had a logo: a large "K," its bottom legs filling a dugout canoe being propelled by two African oarsmen. I had a rubber stamp made of it. Using a red-inked stamp pad, we stamped the logo on the left end of the legal-size envelope. This gave our letters immediate identification.

8. Mail your newsletter at a regular frequency

If you mail a monthly letter, people will attach little significance to it, and will come to ignore it altogether. If you mail it quarterly, it will gain for itself a higher level of interest. If you mail it twice a year, its arrival becomes a more significant event (and your costs are much less!). Maintaining the frequency will earn you the readers' credibility.

9. Periodically update your mailing list

Over most of our years, our mailing list was a box of indexed 3-by-5 inch cards. Whenever we received a letter, we would mark on that person's card the month and year we received it. At the end of a year, we informed our readers that only those we had heard from would be receiving our next newsletter. It was our opinion that a person who had not written us once over the period of a year could hardly be counted upon as a faithful prayer warrior. In more recent years a computer has facilitated our record keeping.

10. Personally answer every personal letter

If you and your spouse are equally occupied with "mission work" and have parenting responsibilities, it may be difficult to find time for this. But it pays rich dividends in terms of prayer support. Your personal letter bonds you to the person receiving it. It is highly valued. Such letters build people's esteem for you. Your mutual exchange of correspondence with such persons over the years builds a kind of lifetime loyalty. Your faithfulness in answering their letters guarantees you their faithful prayer support.

Another means of strengthening your bond to the home church is by exchanging videos. You may want to first write to someone in your church proposing the idea. Ask where such a video might best be used, and how long it should be. Your pastor may invite you to send a 10-minute video to be included in a Sunday morning worship service. A Sunday School teacher may want a 20-minute video with a specific age-group focus. The leader of a home Bible study group may invite you to submit a half-hour video to play at their Wednesday night meeting. In turn, when people have finished using the video, they can delegate someone to videotape a morning worship service, and return the video to you. If you do not have a camcorder available, you can prepare a set of slides with narration on cassette. What you record must be pertinent and interesting, or the result will be disappointing.

Fax or e-mail, if available, make it possible for you to quickly inform people in your home church of an emergency prayer need, or to update them on your current prayer needs. If funds are available, and you have phone service, coordinating a phone call to your home church at the time of a worship service or missions conference is especially effective.

Taking the time necessary to maintain strong relationships with the home church is indispensable to a missionary's fulfilling her or his potential.

16

The Missionary's Support System

The primary purpose of a mission agency is to facilitate people doing mission work. The agency's policies and functions are determined by a board which meets once or twice a year. The board delegates its authority to an executive secretary (the CEO) and his (or her) coterie of assistants who work five days a week at an office carrying the agency's name and address.

As a missionary candidate, your relationship to a mission board is analogous to a courtship: occasional contacts by which you become increasingly acquainted, followed by an extended period when the relationship becomes increasingly personal and bonding. But always with the understanding that the relationship may be terminated at any point without further obligation to either party.

As a missionary, your decision to serve under a given mission board might be seen as a marriage: you enter into a covenant relationship to work under said board for better or for worse; and for so long as your career shall last. In the meanwhile, incompatibility that culminates in separation carries with it the price of pain.

Every mission agency has a policy manual. Read it thoroughly. First, study the board's doctrinal statement. Next, the mission agency's policy in regards to raising money for your support. Such policies are best viewed along a spectrum. On one end of the spectrum is the support arrangement of larger mainline denominations. Part of the money assessed from each of the denomination's churches is designated for missions. This arrangement has advantages, in that the missionary does not have to do deputation work to raise and maintain his support; it is guaranteed by his denominational mission board. However, this arrangement is impersonal, in that the missionary has little direct contact with people in the congregation. And they, in giving to the denomination's annual budget, are not highly motivated to support a line item designated for missions.

On the opposite end of the spectrum is the "faith" mission. It has neither identification with, nor support by a denomination. Candidates raise their own support. They appeal for help from congregations by means of deputation traveling. This arrangement also has advantages. It brings the missionary into direct contact with people in many congregations. People are motivated to give, because they know personally the missionary they are supporting.

On the other hand, this arrangement can be very time consuming. A missionary's departure date may be postponed for 18 months or two years, pending the raising of adequate support. The support base of a missionary family may be divided between 30 widely scattered churches. When this family comes home for furlough, a primary concern is to maintain their support base. Much of their time will be spent traveling to visit their supporting churches, robbing them of time to rest and recuperate for another term of service.

What items a monthly support figure includes also vary widely with different agencies. Does the figure cover only your personal living costs? Is this enough for a lifestyle on the field that is healthy and reasonably comfortable? Does it include medical costs? Monthly Social Security premiums? Retirement benefits? Does it include costs for your ministry? Does it include a subsidy to help support missionaries who are part of your team, but who come from less affluent countries? Is provision made for your allowance to be adjusted with the inflation index of a country? If not, in a country where inflation rises 10 percent monthly, you may soon go hungry.

For example, a mission agency known for its frugal use of funds requires a missionary couple to raise monthly support of $2,000 for the husband-wife team, $125 per child ages 0-5, and $1,000 for ministry. It has an in-house medical plan to which each missionary contributes, no retirement benefits, but a home for retired missionaries needing personal care.

Do all the agency's missionaries on a given field receive the same allowance, or is a missionary permitted to keep and use whatever amount donors send him? In the latter case, a more articulate, personable missionary may enjoy a generous monthly allowance, while a colleague who is less articulate but is doing a work just as significant, endures financial hardship. Such a situation does not foster positive interpersonal relationships.

In the same vein, what is the board's policy regarding personal ownership of equipment deemed important for facilitating one's ministry?

A candidate missionary doctor prepares to go to Brazil. He shares his concern that his medical ministry on the field bring people to Christ. His philanthropic colleagues give him funds to purchase a portable motor-generator, a P. A. system, a movie projector, and films. He goes to the field, and enjoys an effective ministry.

However, the missionary working under the same board on the same field whose designated work is evangelism does not have well-heeled colleagues to buy him such equipment. On the field, he carries out his duties faithfully, but on a much lower profile.

Nationals in Brazil ask the doctor, "Where did you get the money for all that equipment?"

"The Lord gave it to me," the doctor will reply.

Nationals ask the evangelist, "Why don't you have equipment to do evangelism like the doctor has?"

"I don't have money to buy it," the missionary evangelist replies.

"Then why don't you ask the doctor to loan you his equipment? Aren't you both members of God's family?"

"Oh, no. I could never do that. He bought those things

with his money. If something broke while I was using it, how could I repair it?"

"Strange," the Brazilian nationals muse. "The Lord gives a doctor money to do evangelism, and leaves the evangelist a pauper. They're both Christians, but they won't share their things. So the doctor is the big evangelist, and the evangelist is a little evangelist. And they teach us to love one another, and that the Lord is no respecter of persons."

The same principle applies regarding the private ownership of vehicles. The missionary is observed to have money to get a new car. The missionary says, "God gave it to me." Nationals notice that for some missionaries, "God provides" two cars. For others, God "doesn't provide" very well, because they drive a dilapidated car term after term. Nationals take the missionaries' explanation with a grain of salt. If "God provides," why doesn't he provide equally? Why doesn't he also "provide" cars for nationals?

To avoid such confusion, many mission boards require supervising the purchase of equipment. The missionary evangelist would explain to the board his need for audio visual equipment. The board would consider his request, and likely approve it as a "special project." The board then joins forces with the evangelist to raise money to purchase the equipment and send it to the field. The missionary doctor's request for similar equipment would not be considered until the evangelist is already using his equipment to expand his ministry.

Similarly, the board will consider the request of the missionary evangelist for a motor vehicle to use in his work of evangelism. It will consider the request of a missionary doctor for a vehicle to enable him to conduct rural clinics. In either case, if a vehicle is purchased, it belongs to the mission, and not to the individual. Where a number of mission vehicles are operating from a common base on the field, one person is officially charged with maintaining and repairing them.

On the field, finances easily become an issue of contention. The problems can be reduced if guidelines are given in a policy manual.

17

Choosing the Right Mission Board

Faith mission boards have played a paramount role in the growth of the modern global missionary enterprise. But you should be aware of some smaller boards which publish attractively lean operating budgets, but tell only part of the story.

Missionaries from such a board have been known to arrive unexpectedly on a field where other missions have long-established work, and announce, "God has given us a vision to begin work in this field." They operate by fiat of a presumed "divine right."

They disregard policies established between the earlier missions. They proselyte national believers and leaders away from already existing churches.

The situations which follow are not postulated; they exist. While such missions operate independently, they depend heavily on larger, well-established missions for their support systems. They have no vacation or retreat facilities; so they'll go rest as guests at a station of a larger mission. Or they may show up without prior notice, expecting their hosts to make whatever provisions needed for their staying overnight.

Some such mission agencies merely assume that places will be made for their missionaries' children in the area's jointly operated school for missionaries' children, though the agencies have inadequate resources to contribute to the school's operating costs or staff.

Missionaries of such boards will ask to purchase gasoline, kerosene, and diesel fuel from a larger neighboring mission. They do not have funds for ordering their own fuel in quantity. When problems of visa renewal occur, they will ask a larger neighboring mission to intercede for them, because they have no one designated as a "legal representative."

When missionaries of such agencies are back home doing deputation work, one hears nothing about their operating on the field by means of a borrowed support system. One only hears how the Lord has miraculously provided all their needs. Their posture of unashamed dependency seems to reflect the Buddhists' philosophy: "It is to your benefit that you help us, because it will increase your stature in the next level of life."

They have no reserve financial credit on the field, so when a missionary becomes ill and needs an emergency trip home, they will ask other missions to lend them money for travel costs.

In Zaire, where we worked, a single lady missionary had recurring attacks of cerebral malaria until she lost her mind. Her mission had neither money nor personnel to assist her. She was placed alone on a river steamer for a five-day trip downstream to the capital city of Kinshasa. There she was hospitalized, placed in a straitjacket, and tended by empathetic missionaries of other agencies until arrangements were made for her flight home at United States government expense.

What is the mission board's attitude regarding mental illness? There are still those boards who don't believe missionaries should be victims of such illness. Missionaries who develop such problems simply "lack spiritual dedication." They are summarily dropped from the roster, because "they don't have the necessary qualifications."

By the second term of service, the missionary has come to rely heavily upon the mission board as the primary part of her support. When I suffered clinical depression, my most haunting fear was of being abandoned. If, at such a point, my mission board washes its hands of any further responsibility for me, the major part of my support structure disintegrates. This would grease my slide into despair. On the other hand, if my mission board comes alongside me and does whatever it can to facilitate my recovery, I will feel forever indebted to it.

Many mission boards do the Lord's work. But not all of them do it wisely and responsibly. "Court" your prospective mission board sagaciously. Are you in agreement with the age that your agency mandates that children leave home for boarding school? Does the agency allow you to be involved in peace and social issues in a manner that is compatible with your understanding of Scripture?

Is annual vacation mandated? It should be. Sometimes a missionary feels his work is so important that it cannot survive his two-week absence for vacation. But his marathon loyalty eventually makes him a lion to live with.

Does the agency have a fixed period for field service followed by a fixed period at home "on furlough" (or on "home assignment")? Does it cover your living costs while you are at home? Are you guaranteed at least four months of a one-year furlough for complete rest, or will the travel demands of deputation be so continuous that you have very little time for recuperation?

Is the mission board open to making an exception to the rule to meet a missionary's specific need? Sometimes an elderly parent needs care. Or children need the stability of parental supervision during certain years of their schooling. Or you need additional specialized education to improve your ministry skills. During such periods of extended furlough, does the board stop payment of your monthly support, or does it collaborate with you in maintaining it?

We served two terms in Zaire. By then, the need for preparing Christian literature in our major tribal language was urgent. This was a need I wanted to address. Our mission board granted us a two-year furlough, with monthly allowance guaranteed. It allowed me to accept invitations for conducting evangelistic or spiritual renewal services, and use the honoraria towards covering my study costs. I earned a graduate degree in journalism. This equipped me not only for subsequent ministry in literature production and distribution overseas; it gave me a professional skill I could use for the rest of my life.

At another point in our career, we took a five-year extended furlough in order to provide our children needed stability in a home environment. The board helped me find employment in our denominational bookstore, and Eudene worked part-time as a nurse. Our salaries went to remunerate our monthly living allowance. Our medical coverage, Social Security, and pension payments were not interrupted.

Such flexibility in time of personal need is deeply appreciated. Making such exceptions often imposes inconvenient schedule adjustments upon others. Some smaller mission boards are unwilling, or unable, to make such adjustments. On the other hand, a friend of mine serves under a large mission board that rigidly adheres to its rules; any flexibility may set a dangerous precedent. Every child must leave for school at age six. Every missionary must be back on the field at the end of his or her 12th furlough month.

You cannot predict the variety of situations you will encounter while overseas. Frequently, your mission board's policy will determine how you are allowed to respond to them. For example, a single missionary may discover the blossoming of romance. What is the mission board's policy in regards to her marrying a coworker, or a national? What if you wish to adopt an orphan? Or buy real estate overseas as an investment? Or undertake a business venture to supplement your monthly allowance?

The growing chasm between the rich and the poor fosters increasing political instability on a global scale. Missionaries who serve in countries where there is great disparity of wealth are increasingly caught in settings of political unrest and revolution. Occasionally missionaries are kidnapped and held hostage. In Chapter 13 I recounted our personal experience during a period of revolution.

This growing destabilization has made it necessary for mission boards to formulate contingency plans to be implemented, should such conditions affect their missionaries and work. What preparations should missionaries make in advance to be better prepared for such an eventuality? What criteria must prevail to make withdrawal advisable? Who decides when these criteria are met? What are the specific procedures for withdrawal? Are there documents that need to be destroyed before missionaries evacuate? What items are important for missionaries to take with them?

Should they carry arms? How much luggage is each person allowed? Are routes of escape defined and prioritized? If orderly evacuation is possible, who is to leave first, and who is to stay the longest? What is the board's policy regarding negotiating for the release of kidnapped missionaries?

You should know in advance your board's policy on all such issues; they bear directly upon your safety and welfare. Then, should you be caught in a politically destabilized situation, misunderstanding and pain will be minimized.

18

The Consequences of Overwork

Michael felt called of God to missionary service from an early age. He arrived in Africa at Telekolo Mission Station. He founded a vocational school and gave himself heart and soul to making it a success. He hired nationals to the teaching staff. The school thrived. At the beginning of its second year, Betty, a single missionary, came and joined the school's staff. By this time, Michael's work pace was wearing him down. Relational problems with his national staff developed. Then a government official visited the school. He left Michael a long list of improvements to be made if the school was to qualify for a 50 percent subsidy towards covering its operating costs. One mid-morning Michael found Betty drinking coffee at the home of Tom and Dianne, a couple about her age.

"I'm carrying a big load to make this school work," he addressed her. "I need to see that other people on my staff are as committed as I am."

"What makes you feel I'm not as committed as you are?" Betty rejoined.

"Because you're sitting here drinking coffee. This time of day you ought to be in your office."

"Can't we take a coffee break?"

"You not only take time for a coffee break. In the afternoons, you always leave your office long before I do."

"I don't do all my work at the office. I take work home. Often I have appointments with students at home."

"Well, it's not a good example for the national staff," Michael scolded. "They'll be taking more time off their work than is acceptable. I wish you did your work and had your appointments at school so I knew what is going on."

"Michael, you're finding your load very heavy, aren't you?" Tom empathized.

"Yes," he agreed. "Directing this school is just too much work for one person to handle."

"Why don't you call a meeting of the school board, and ask them to appoint a national to help you?"

Subsequently the school board appointed Loshi, a young man who had demonstrated gifts of administration on a church staff, to serve as administrative assistant to Michael. Then the sphere of Michael's relational problems grew to include Loshi.

One day during the second semester Michael went to Russell and Sarah, senior missionaries at Telekolo Mission Station. He told them of his increasing difficulties with his staff, and of his mounting stress.

"Michael, you seem very tired," Sarah remarked. "Are you sleeping well at night?"

"No. I can't get all this stuff out of my mind. Even after lunch every day, when all the rest of you are enjoying a siesta, I can't. People are on the path outside my apartment chattering, and kids are playing under the mango tree just outside my yard. If this noise isn't taken care of, I'm going to resign. It's simply too much for me to bear."

Russell took the issue to the local church council. The council agreed to hire a sentry. Money would be taken from the contingency fund to pay him. His job was to keep things quiet outside Michael's apartment from noon until 2 p.m. The man sat on a chair at the corner of Michael's yard with a switch in his hand. He kept people off the path and chased children away from the mango tree.

One evening Michael came to see Russell and Sarah. He was angry. "Loshi wants to get rid of me," he announced.

"What makes you say that?" Russell asked.

"Because he's plotting to replace me."

"Michael, you're hallucinating," Sarah reacted. "You

need a rest."

"So your thinking is just like all the rest of them! I thought so. You're all against me. Nobody understands."

"I'll call Loshi tomorrow and talk with him," Russell said.

During the three-month dry-season break, Michael went to visit a friend in the city. Meanwhile, the school board designated Loshi to work alongside Michael as co-director for a one-year period, at the end of which Loshi would become director of the vocational school. This was part of the board's plan of "Africanization": nationals taking over leading positions now held by missionaries. When Michael returned, Russell informed him of the decision.

"It will never work," Michael remonstrated.

"Why?" Russell asked.

Michael began recounting a long list of reasons why the plan was untenable.

"Why couldn't Betty co-direct the school with me?" he asked. "We get along pretty well."

"I don't think there's much chance of that," Russell replied. "If you're not in agreement with the plan, you'll have to take the issue back to the school board."

Michael called a special meeting of the school board. Everybody agreed that the decision should not be changed.

"That proves what I've been suspecting," Michael replied. "You've been plotting all along to get rid of me. Your unwillingness to consider changing your decision proves it. There's nothing left for me to do but resign."

"But we still need you," the chairman explained. "Loshi needs a year of training so that the transition will be smooth."

"I don't care about the transition," Michael retorted. "I'm quitting. You'll find the keys to the school on my office desk in the morning. Tomorrow I'll ask the field chairman to begin making plans for my return to the States."

Michael is a composite of several missionaries I have known, including myself at one point in time. What measures can missionaries take to better assure their health and well-being?

19

Maintaining Personal Wholeness

Like Michael, a missionary may cut herself off from others, surrender herself into the gaping maw of need, and pursue that course to the inevitable end of burnout. But I do not believe such a sacrifice is "holy and pleasing unto God" (Rom. 12:1 NIV). We glorify God not with our brokenness, but with our wholeness. To maintain that wholeness, I offer the following eight suggestions.

1. I need to foster supportive social relationships.

Abandoning myself to work is to concur with a fallacious assumption in our culture that ultimate happiness is found in production. A job well done does bring satisfaction. God "produced" the world, and said, "It is good." But he found the product itself incomplete. He then created man and woman in his image in order to enjoy fellowship. This suggests that ultimate happiness lies not in our production, but in our social relationships.

In very practical terms, this means I take time to enjoy my spouse; to do fun things with my children. It means inviting nationals to our home for a meal, or inviting other missionaries to come for an evening of parlor games and refreshments. I remember when we missionaries regularly stockpiled ice cubes in our kerosene refrigerators until we could make a freezer of hand-churned ice cream.

2. I need to work at maintaining a personal attitude that invites the formation of such relationships.

In times of conflict I need to restrain my emotions; I should not take sides. I will not criticize. I will not gossip. When I am wronged, I may defend the truth in love, but I dare not return evil for evil. I must forgive quickly and totally, and keep my memory swept clean of grudges. My words and deeds must demonstrate that I care about others at least as much as I care for myself. When I fail to measure up (as I did), I should be the first to admit it.

3. When possible, I should break my job down into bite-sized pieces.

This enables me to set goals for myself that are challenging but achievable. When a goal is achieved, I can afford to congratulate myself by enjoying some little ritual of celebration, like baking a cake and inviting someone over for tea; or taking a break in my schedule for a hike into the woods.

4. Have a wide range of interests from which I can draw satisfaction.

My location may not allow me to pursue all of them, but it will some of them. For example, I may enjoy hiking, nature, stamp collecting, reading, and music. (Over the years my library became my treasure chest, from which, at will, I could draw the kind of lode I found pleasurable at that time.) If I am located on an isolated mission station, my pursuing an interest in music will not include attending symphony concerts. But I can enjoy a recorded concert from a CD or a phonograph disk. Or, I can play my own musical instrument. I learned that evenings should be set aside for such diversions, and not for extending my workday.

5. Maintain flexibility in my schedule.

I should not view my daily agenda as inviolable. It should allow me enough space to roll with the punches. I can be like Michael, whose program controlled him. Or, I can be in charge of my program, but control it too rigidly. It's best if, while controlling my program, I maintain a component of flexibility which allows me to temporarily put my agenda on hold. That way, if I decide to take an early morning bird-watching walk, I can do it. If neighbors ask me to join them on a late-afternoon picnic, I can go.

6. Have an adequate self-image.

This comes from a knowledge that is rooted in certain facts about God. He made me as he did for a purpose. This means that whatever service I offer him is valued and unique. I can enjoy myself as I am, and have no reason for trying to be someone else. I try to imagine myself as standing in an uninterrupted flow of love that springs from God.

7. Maintaining a daily retreat with God.

For many years on the field, my work activities began at 8 a.m. I got up at 5:30 and had an hour of quiet time with God before breakfast at 7. Normally, my retreat time is divided between prayer and reading or studying the Bible. Part of my prayer time is spent in silent meditation. While in prayer, I do not struggle to maintain a continuous focus upon God. I allow my mind freedom to encompass the day's challenges. Often I get fresh insights for meeting them. I see these insights as a gift from God. I jot them down while they are fresh and clear.

It's important that time spent with the Bible remain interesting and instructive. This may mean changing my Bible activity from time to time. For years, I followed a daily calendar whereby I completed reading the Bible in a year. Currently, I read a passage, along with notes from a voluminous commentary explaining it.

8. Take a yearly vacation.

Its primary purpose should be my recuperation. Keeping this objective in mind will help determine the vacation's length and its activities. Within the limits of my budget, what activity (or inactivity) would I find genuinely recreative? One must guard against excess. For example, if I find travel recreative, I shouldn't overload my schedule. If I do, I will come home still weary, and flagellating myself for having squandered my opportunity to recuperate.

As you will see in the next chapter, once I did not adequately heed these admonitions, and paid for it dearly.

20

Depression

Depression is the enemy of relationships. It shifts life's focus away from others' needs to my own needs.

In 1980 Eudene developed a health condition that did not allow us to return overseas. I felt that the next best thing to being a missionary was to train others to become missionaries. At age 55 I earned a graduate degree qualifying me to teach missions. Wide circulation of my resume turned up one job opening in a small Bible College in the far Northwest, 2,300 miles away. In August of 1984 we packed all our earthly belongings into a big U-Haul truck, and relocated from Fort Wayne, Indiana, to British Columbia, Canada.

I eagerly took up this new challenge. I researched, designed courses, prepared daily lesson plans, taught. Then doubts began eroding my self-confidence. I was a preacher. I was a writer. But who ever said I was a teacher? Could I at my age communicate with kids just out of high school? If I did not win tenure at the end of my first year of teaching, how would we continue our house mortgage payments? How would I handle failure?

I worked harder, to reinforce my self-worth, to gain assurance that I would succeed. Then gnawing doubts would recycle the sequence. Ultimately, these gnawing doubts came home and went to bed with me. They began hindering my sleep. Because of inadequate sleep, my daily routine challenges became increasingly unmanageable. By 3 p.m. they would loom before me like a range of insurmountable mountains, incapacitating me to continue. My nights became long terrifying hours of wakefulness that would not surrender to sedatives. Like Michael, I became psychotic.

I sought the help of a Christian psychiatrist. He counselled me weekly. My stressed state of mind and my seeming lack of progress once prompted me to suggest that my problem could be demonic. His response indicated to me that helping me was beyond the sphere of his skills. I stopped seeing him.

Fears of demonic assault erode one's faith in God. Soon the spectres of ugly sins of my past were haunting me. Had God ever really blotted them out? Would he? Two devout, understanding friends heard my confession. One of them put his hand on my knee, claimed the promise of Matthew 18:18, 19, and pronounced me forgiven. That problem was resolved.

I could not understand what was happening to me at the time, but now, in retrospect, I can plot my descent into depression: 1) gnawing fear that I would fail in my new assignment; 2) a growing inability to cope with the daily challenges of life; 3) losing my grip on faith that I was loved and forgiven by God; and 4) fatigue from loss of sleep that pressed me to desperation.

Eudene and I went for another visit with my physician. I informed him that the most recent sedative was no longer effective. "Doctor," I added, "You've got to do something to help me. I feel like I'm going to explode into a thousand pieces."

He fixed his gaze on me, pondered, and said, "Mr. Keidel, we will put you in a place where you will find help." He showed me to a counter where I signed myself into the hospital's psychiatric ward.

I was taken to my room, and went to bed. I awakened about midnight. I got up to look out of the window glass. The panes were reinforced with fine-mesh wire. Then it struck me: I was locked inside this place. I was imprisoned. I began pacing the floor and fulminating: "I've failed the college, my students, the president. I've failed Eudene. I've failed Mom and Dad. I've failed God. I've failed everybody."

The night nurse came to calm me. My mind was black as night. In it I saw the two red tail lights of a big loaded U-Haul truck headed back to Fort Wayne, Indiana.

After about 10 days on heavy medication, my reasoning powers returned to the point where I could profit from counselling. For an hour every day, a psychiatric nurse worked with me. This attention alone helped convince me that I was a person of worth. I came to hold these nurses in the highest regard. They build a bridge of understanding whereby the mentally ill return to the world of sanity. Their professional skills provided insights I needed to reach some very important conclusions.

"Levi, you are a very angry man," they insisted. "What do you mean?" I protested. I didn't sense that I was angry with anyone. Eventually I came to understand that it was true. My four siblings and I grew up during the Depression years. Our parents had their hands full feeding and clothing us. They had little time to show us love and affirmation. As a child I concluded that, while I apparently had little intrinsic worth as a person, I could prove I was worthy of their love by hard work. Neither did my hard work earn their tokens of love. However, it did set me onto a lifelong course of driving myself, to assure me that I was a person of worth, and to show God I was a person worthy of his love. Now, at age 59, my drivenness institutionalized me, and I carried anger baggage that resulted from my having been denied the parental affection I felt I deserved during my childhood years.

Counselors helped me deal with my anger. They helped me learn that self-worth is intrinsic to me as a human being. It is neither improved by my works, nor lessened by lack of them. I could make my personal salvation no more secure by proving to God that I deserved it. The recognition of this fact defused my drivenness. I could relax, and enjoy life for its relationships rather than for its achievements. This introduced me to a slower-paced lifestyle.

At the end of a month I was released from the hospital. Eudene was saying, "I have a new husband." My children told each other, "Dad is a different man." And to end for-

ever the devil's sowing doubts about my personal salvation,
I planted myself squarely on the claims of an old gospel
song:

> My hope is built on nothing less
> Than Jesus' blood and righteousness.
> I dare not trust the sweetest frame;
> But wholly lean on Jesus' name.
> His oath, His covenant, His blood,
> Support me in the whelming flood;
> When all around my soul gives way,
> He then is all my hope and stay.
> On Christ the solid rock I stand;
> All other ground is sinking sand,
> All other ground is sinking sand.[1]

---

1. Lyric by Edward Mote, c. 1834; music by William Batchelder
Bradbury, 1863.

21

Friction with the Spouse

As I've mentioned before, Eudene was raised in a warm and caring Christian home. My parents raised us five children during the depression. Mom and Dad were sharecroppers. They worked their fingers to the bone. There was always ample food on the table. Discipline was strict. Because the bottom line was survival, our parents didn't have time to affirm us. They didn't acknowledge special effort. One time I asked them why, when I did a good job, they never said "Thank you." The answer: "We're afraid you'll get the big head." I needed signs of their love and approval. To get those signs, I strove for perfection.

I was converted at age 18. Later, I met Eudene. We both felt called to serve God, were married, and undertook our missionary career in Africa. It would be great if, when a guy and girl are dating, they could ask each other, "What are your idiosyncrasies? Give me a list of them." Then they could decide whether they wanted to begin adjusting to each other, or to just call it quits. Unfortunately, it doesn't work that way. Making those adjustments is a lifelong process. Eudene and I had no idea how our dissimilar upbringings would cause friction in our relationships.

According to an understanding among "ordinary Christians," missionaries "wear haloes." I drove myself to fulfill the stereotype. I overworked. Whenever we returned to the States for furlough, I was so burned out that it took more than the authorized year for me to recoup energy and begin feeling positive about returning to the field.

All this was to assure myself that I was a success. I pressured my wife and children to reinforce my success image. When I corrected Eudene, she took it as a put-down. She would say, "I can never do anything right." If I did not get ego strokes from other people, surely I could expect them from my wife. But the defense of her own personal identity did not allow her to give them. This angered me.

In 1977, during our 29th year of marriage, Eudene and I began to notice a recurring pattern. We would reciprocate unkind remarks. Then, having wounded each other, we did not know how to gracefully back off from each other. On one such occasion I said, "It's time for us to seek help." Over Eudene's reservations, I arranged an appointment for us at a mental health center.

Counsellors concluded that Eudene was the mentally healthy person. I was motivated by some undefinable drivenness. "Levi," they said, "you need a fresh experience of the grace of God." And where, I mused, do I get that? They recommended we attend a weeklong marriage enrichment seminar. On the way to it, we debated if the results would warrant the 300-mile travel costs.

At the seminar we learned helpful conflict resolution techniques. For example, we learned how to depersonalize hurts. A wife could complain, "Why do you always leave your dirty socks on the floor?" Or, she could say, "I really find it difficult to keep the bedroom in order when I keep finding dirty socks on the floor." A husband might complain, "Why do you always scatter the newspaper all over the carpet when you're done reading it?" Or, he could say, "When I want to read the newspaper, it upsets me to have to put together the pieces that have been scattered on the carpet."

But on the final day something far more significant happened. Each enrolled couple in turn was required to sit facing each other. They were to engage in an inventory dialogue on their marriage relationship, while counsellors listened. When our turn came, Eudene and I began following our prepared agenda. Soon Mary, Eudene's counsellor, began getting strong vibes of Eudene's subconscious hurts. Our agenda was abandoned. Leslie, my counsellor, coached me in active listening: responding to Eudene in a manner that would encourage her to openly express herself. I felt highly intimidated to give Eudene such freedom. I realized I was surrendering my authority over her; and this meant I was relinquishing control over my self-image. I mouthed the coached responses over the protests of my brain. Encouraged by hearing my empathetic responses, Eudene ultimately dumped a 29-year-old gunny sack filled with putdowns.

"This kind of record could be grounds for divorce," Mary said.

I had no recourse but to admit my failures to Eudene, and ask her to forgive me. Mary asked Eudene, "How do you feel?"

"About 10 feet tall," she replied.

What were the interacting relational factors that over the years had created such a situation? Eudene grew up with parents whose mutual relationship was adult-to-adult. When we were married, I feared Eudene would seek to control me. To preclude this, I took an authoritarian posture and controlled her, as adult to child. While Eudene was totally unfamiliar with such a husband-wife relationship, she meekly submitted to it, gunny-sacking her hurts in order to save our marriage. I had no idea of the fearful toll I was exacting from her. I was withholding from her human wholeness. As Scott Peck observes:

> It is possible to kill, or attempt to kill. . . without actually destroying the body. . . Erich Fromm was acutely sensitive to this fact when he broadened the definition of necrophilia to include the desire of certain people to control others—to foster their dependency, to discourage their capacity to think for themselves, to diminish their unpredictability and originality, to keep them in line. . . (one whose) aim is to (transform) others into obedient automatons, robbing them of their humanity.[1]

Eudene summed up this marriage enrichment experience as a "second honeymoon." Now that I had freed her to be a person in her own right, she no longer felt the need to "get even" by denying me her affirmation. Our relationship entered an era of unprecedented growth. There have been occasional glitches since then, but we are able to talk about them and resolve them. Reflecting back on our 47 years of married life, and upon the compatibility we now enjoy, I wonder if all the bumps and bruises were necessary for us to reach this point.

One thing that will put a whole new perspective on your marriage is a separation from your spouse imposed upon the two of you by your mutual commitment to Christ.

---

1. M. Scott Peck. *People of the Lie* (New York: Simon and Schuster, Inc., 1983) 42-43.

22

Family Separation

J esus' most stringent demands for discipleship focused on the bonds of family: "If anyone comes to me and does not hate his father and mother, his wife and children, his brothers and sisters. . .he cannot be my disciple." (Lk. 14:26 NIV). Eudene and I found that the rewards of missionary service far outweigh the sacrifices. But its most stringent demand likely will be separation from members of the family.

The missionary candidate will first encounter the issue when she informs her parents of her plans for serving the Lord overseas. If her parents are not Christians, they may outright object to her going. Or they may ridicule her for "throwing away your life." Under such circumstances, her departure from them and her extended separation from them will mean dealing with a high level of stress.

Even Christian parents may hinder her. Frequently they say, "It's all right for other people's children, but not for ours." If the daughter goes overseas anyhow, she will have to accept stress-laden relationships with her parents.

My parents were young believers when, one Sunday noon at the dinner table, I asked what they would think, should I become an overseas missionary. There was a long silence. Then Mom said, "Well, if that's what you believe the Lord wants you to do, then you'd better do it." Years later she explained the span of silence. "When you were 18 months old, you were very ill. The doctor said you had a 50 percent chance of survival. When I was alone, I kneeled by my bed and promised the Lord that if he let me keep my boy, he could do whatever he wanted to with him. I forgot my promise for 17 years, until that noon when you asked me that question."

How fortunate are the missionaries who are sent forth with their parents' blessing! The letters exchanged regularly during their separation will be warm with sharing, caring, and affirmation.

A missionary mother will better understand the poignant feelings of her parents when she first left home, at a later point in time: when she watches her own children leave for boarding school. This is likely the greatest sacrifice missionaries are called upon to make. Some mission agencies require that children be sent to boarding school at age six; other agencies at ages eight or nine. The older the child, the less trauma will be suffered by both parents and child.

Packing your child off to boarding school would be somewhat less stressful if you had some clue as to how the experience was going to affect your child. Our oldest daughter arrived at boarding school, cried for a few nights, and then adjusted rapidly to school routine. Her roommate cried herself to sleep every night for 10 weeks. The only way parents have to help children deal with such stresses of separation is by letter, or in more favorable circumstances, by telephone. Sometimes parents hurt deeply because of the inadequacy of these means. At such times, they will lean heavily upon the competence of dormitory house parents and boarding-school teachers to fill the role of surrogate parents, and upon prayer.

But in most cases, boarding school becomes a rewarding and happy experience. Missionary children are normal, resourceful kids, able to adapt to their new situations in creative ways. Once a doctor's small son found access to a large bottle of good-tasting pills. He curried friendship by passing them around to his classmates as candy. Several had to have their stomachs pumped. Our son confessed to "underground trading." He would rub an impressive-looking white "salve" on the scratches and minor sores of Africans in trade for a handful of field peanuts. He ate them as a between-class snack. Eudene and I never recognized that he was using an unusual amount of toothpaste.

Then comes the day when your oldest child graduates from high school, and must return overseas to begin college. Normally, other missionaries who are going home for furlough will travel with him to the homeland, and deposit him on a college campus. (Our son, more adventuresome than many, went home alone, via Spain, fulfilling his wish to buy a guitar and see a bullfight.) Now the stresses of separation are intensified by geographic distance because it takes longer to exchange letters, and phone calls are costly, if possible at all.

How do you respond when you learn that he is finding it intolerable to live with his roommate? Or his academic grades suffer because of his greater love for sports? Or when a month after his arrival he has fallen head-over-heels in love with the kind of girl he felt he would never discover this side of heaven? You strongly suspect that their bond is mutual loneliness, hardly an adequate basis upon which to build a permanent relationship. Should you share with your son your serious reservations about the relationship? If he should follow your advice, and break off with her, then never afterwards discover another girl who compared with her, who would he blame for his unhappiness for the rest of his life? If you fail to express your sincere reservations, and your suspicions are validated by a subsequent divorce, how will you justify yourself for not having raised a flag of caution? How do you process your guilt? One can feel totally disempowered by the factor of separation.

Sometimes situations arise where missionary spouses are required to temporarily separate. In the early years of our missionary career, a couple decided that educational needs of their children necessitated their separation for two years, he in Africa doing the Lord's work, and she in the States with the children. That requires heroic dedication.

During our last term in Zaire, doctors agreed that Eudene should return to the States for major surgery; it would require a three-month separation. I focused my attention on maintaining my ability to function normally during the span of her absence. I initiated daily late-afternoon disciplines of jogging and practicing my violin, to distract me from loneliness.

My first big challenge came when I ran out of bread. We had no bakery. Eudene had left me the bread-making recipe. I was at the kitchen counter combining ingredients in a large mixing bowl. At my right elbow was Lusambu, our congenial house helper. He was observing this marvel.

The process stopped; my eyes began scanning all the cupboard shelves.

"What are you looking for?" he asked.

"Our metal measuring cup."

He took it off the shelf just left of my eye level and gave it to me.

"That's just what Mama said would happen," he volunteered.

"What?"

"She said before she went to America that because you study your books in the office so much, part of your brain has been ruined and we have to loan you our eyes."

Some days later an African leader from a distance stopped by to pray for me. The Zaire language of our area has the word "tshitaku" (chee-tah-koo), which means the heavy part of an object, like the heavier end of a large stick used for tamping earth around a post, or that part where the bulk rests; it also means a buttock. We bowed our heads, and he said: "God, I pray to you for this man. His tshitaku has gone across the big water to get fixed. What is a house without a tshitaku? Take care of his tshitaku until it comes back again, so that this can be a complete house again."

He was paying tribute to the importance of my wife. But my translation of the word told me that, though she had been gone for less than six weeks, already my brain was damaged, and I had no rear end.

I needed all the prayers possible. At times my loneliness left me feeling like an empty bowl scraped dry. I had to tell myself that, while I yearned body and spirit for Eudene, she was not God, and that my ability to endure came from faith in him, and not from thoughts of her.

Separation leaves one feel most powerless when one learns that overseas a family member has died. My sister and my father died at separate times, while I was overseas. The news arrived by cablegram or radio. First I denied it. Then the truth, as it sank in, brought grief that weakened and destabilized me. For a few days I was unable to perform my regular tasks. Then came a slow and painful wrenching of the bonds we had enjoyed, until they were broken. This prepared me to emotionally release the person, recognizing that we would never see each other on earth again.

These are not easy things to write about. But they are issues which must be faced by the career missionary. Unless the grief of separation is processed, it may help provoke a more serious problem somewhere in the future.

23

Safeguarding Bonds of Family

Missionary couples with children are caught in a bind: meeting the expectations of their home supporters in regards to ministry on the one hand, and fulfilling obligations to their children on the other. This can be particularly difficult for the wife. Home supporters, or her agency, may expect her to be a full-time missionary as well as a mother. If she is primarily occupied with "mission work," her children bear the consequences of inadequate parenting. The problem is compounded if the work of the husband keeps him away from home much of the time, leaving the primary job of rearing children upon her shoulders.

It is well-documented that full-time employment for a mother of small children is inadvisable in our American setting because it jeopardizes family relationships and is harmful for the children. By what line of reasoning can we insist that overseas it is not only advisable, but necessary for a mother to be employed full-time if she is going to "be worth" her support money?

Safeguarding bonds to children

A child's early years are the crucial, formative years. Entrusting a small child into the hands of a national baby sitter five days a week may cause the child to begin forming negative feelings about a life work which robs him or her of parental attention. The practice could well serve to enhance feelings of disrespect and rebellion during adolescence.

I recall when Eudene and I woke up to the fact that our four children were growing up under our roof, and we hadn't become deeply acquainted with them. The oldest would be leaving for boarding school in a few years. Then it would be too late to ever get well-acquainted with him. We decided to schedule into our daily programs a time for them alone.

While I was away from home, Eudene would spend evenings reading to them. By the time our children reached early primary school age, she had read all that pertained to them from the 24-volume Grolier's *Book of Knowledge* at least twice. (Today as adults, they all love to read.) I built a swing and slide and sandbox for them. Frequently, on Saturdays I would hike with them across a prairie or to a jungle stream. These activities showed our children in an understandable way that we loved them.

When they were away at boarding school, their longest time at home was summer vacations. We packed those times with fun. We planned cookouts and tours and picnics. We hiked to an idyllic lake secluded in heavily-wooded hills, and camped on its shores. During the day we fished and explored. During the night we lay listening to the strange sounds of the jungle. We played in river rapids. We camped on the shore of an expansive, quiet river and watched a hippo in the moonlight. We dammed up a forest stream to make a swimming hole; then swinging on a vine Tarzan-style from a nearby hillside, we dropped into it. We traveled the complete length of a lake by rowboat, using a stiff 14-foot banana-shaped leaf for a sail.

Then came our last trip from Africa to the U.S. as a family; it was time for our oldest child to stay home for college. We planned a tour. Our board's policy was to cover travel costs of the normal distance home. We bought our own tickets and flew to a city in southeastern Zaire. This put us into the next-higher category of allowed travel distance home. It enabled us to see wild animals in Kenya, visit the pyramids and museum in Cairo, see the Acropolis and Parthenon in Athens, and then fly to Rome. After three days of sightseeing, we rented a car and drove through the Alps in Switzerland, the Black Forest in southern Germany, and to Paris. After several days of sightseeing there, we flew to the States. These experiences showed our children an advantage of being M.K.'s. Sharing these experiences together bonded us strongly as a family, and garnered for us a trove of happy memories.

Safeguarding bonds to family left behind

It is good if the parents and siblings of a missionary can enjoy some recompense for their long periods of separation from him. This can be done in a number of ways. Eudene and I tried to write home weekly. Occasionally, I would write a "Letter to the Family" describing in detail our recent experiences and activities. (This is not to be confused with our prayer letter to supporters.) We would send them a package of slides focusing upon us, our children, and family activities. Sometimes we exchanged visits by means of cassette. Now video cassettes make such visits even more meaningful. When my missionary interests included radio communications, I contacted the States by ham radio. Our mothers faithfully reciprocated by writing us. Eudene's mother had an almost-perfect weekly letter-writing record for all of our 20-plus years overseas.

Family should be given its fair share of attention when the missionary is home on furlough. We felt this required our choosing a furlough residence close to them, until our children began college. The issue becomes more complex when missionaries' parents live at widely separated addresses, and missionaries' children must be enrolled in school.

For one furlough I asked our agency to schedule deputation visits for me across southern Canada to Seattle, and then down the West Coast to Los Angeles. My parents, Eudene, and our children were to drive from Illinois to friends in Tucson, Arizona. Eudene flew to Seattle to join me for the appointments down the coast. We were to take the train from Los Angeles to Tucson, and then drive from there as a family back to Illinois. It was a great idea, had not mumps in Oregon changed our plans!

The number of young people hearing the call of God to career overseas missionary service is declining. Why? Too often, the reason is protecting family bonds. Few parents suggest to a daughter or son the career option of "a missionary." Rather, they want their children to "succeed in the world." When a group of parents compare the achievements of their children, how frequently do they feel proud to declare that their son is "a missionary in Peru"? Some young people fail to heed the call to missionary service because they attach more value to the accumulation of "things"; they yield to the pressures of American consumerism and become part of the "upward mobility" syndrome. "It costs too much" to be a missionary.

On the contrary, Eudene and I feel it would have cost us too much to *not* be missionaries. We all know what Jesus said about "storing up treasure in heaven," and "seeking first the kingdom of God" (Matt. 6:19-21, 31-33). Apart from that, the rewards in the "here and now" are countless. At this point in life, Eudene and I have an extraordinary sense of contentment. If we had our lives to live over again, we would take the same route a second time.

Bibliography

Adams, Jay Edward. *What Do You Do When You Become Depressed?* Nutley, NJ: Presbyterian and Reformed Publishing Company, 1975.

Arkoun, Mohammed. *Rethinking Ismal: Common Questions, Uncommon Answers.* Boulder: Westview Press, 1994.

Bentley, David E., ed. The Boundaries of god: Muslims in Contact with Non-Muslims. Pasadena, Calif.: Zwemer Institute of Muslim Studies, 1993.

Brislin, Richard W, and Yoshida, Tomoko. *Improving Intercultural Interactions: Modules for Cross-cultural Training Programs.* Thousand Oaks: Sage Publications, 1994.

Burak, Patricia. *Crisis Management in a Cross-cultural Setting.* Washington, D.C.: Association for Foreign Student Affairs, 1987.

Burns, Ridge. *The Complete Student Missions Handbook: A Step-by-Step Guide to Your Group Out of the Classroom and Into the Mission Field.* Grand Rapids: Zondervan Publishing House, 1990.

Burron, Arnold, EdD, and Crews, Jerry, MD. *Guaranteed Steps to Managing Stress.* Wheaton: Tyndale House Publishers, Inc., 1986.

de Santa Ana, Julio. *Good News to the Poor: The Challenge of the Poor in the History of the Church.* Maryknoll: Orbis Books, 1979.

Elliston, Edgar J., ed. *Christian Relief and Development: Developing Workers for Effective Ministry.* Dallas: Word Publishing Company, 1989.

Elmer, Duane. *Cross-cultural Conflict: Building Relationships for Effective Ministry.* Downers Grove, Ill.: Intervarsity Press, 1993.

Fowke, Ruth. *Coping With Crisis.* Valley Forge, Pa.: The Judson Press, 1968.

Foyle, Marjorie F. *Overcoming Missionary Stress.* Wheaton, Ill.: Evangelical Missions Information Service, 1987.

Girardi, Guilo. *Faith and Revolution in Nicaragua: Convergence and Contradiction.* Maryknoll, NY: Orbis Books, 1989.

Grigg, Viv. *Companion to the Poor.* Sutherland, Australia: Albatross Books, 1984.

Gudykunst, William B., and Yun Kim, Young, eds. *Readings on Communications with Strangers.* New York: McGraw-Hill, 1992.

Harley, David C. *Preparing to Serve: Training for Cross-cultural Mission.* Pasadena: William Carey Library, 1995.

Hart, Archibald H. *Coping with Depression in the Ministry and Other Helping Professions.* Waco, Tex.: Word Books, 1984.

Hesselgrave, David J. *Communicating Christ Cross-culturally.* Grand Rapids: Zondervan Publishing House, 1981.

Hovey, Kevin G. *Before All Else Fails Read Instructions: A Manual for Cross-cultural Christians.* Brisbane, Australia: Harvest Publications, 1995.

Kane, J. Herbert. *Life and Work on the Mission Field*. Grand Rapids: Baker Book House, 1980.

___ *The Making of a Missionary*. Grand Rapids: Baker Book House, 1975.

Keidel, Levi. *Caught in the Crossfire*. Scottdale, Pa.: Herald Press, 1979.

Kohls, L. Robert. *Survival Kit for Overseas Living: For Americans Planning to Live and Work Abroad*. Yarmouth, Me.: Intercultural Press, Inc., 1984.

Koslow, Diane R., and Salett, Elizabeth Pathy, eds. *Cross Cultures in Mental Health*. Washington, D.C.: Sieter International, 1989.

Kraft, Charles. *Communication Theory for Christian Witness*. Maryknoll N.Y.: Orbis, 1991.

Linthicum, Robert C. *Empowering the Poor*. Monrovia, Calif.: MARC, 1991.

Lyon, Curtis H. *Pressed Down But Not Forgotten: Depression*. Milwaukee: Northwestern Publishing House, 1993.

McFadden, John, ed. *Transcultural Counselling: Bilateral and International Perspectives*. Alexander, Va.: American Counselling Association, 1993.

Randall, Margaret. *Christians in the Nicaraguan Revolution*. Vancouver: New York Star Books, 1983.

Scott, Waldron. *Bring Forth Justice*. Grand Rapids: William B. Eerdmans, 1980.

Segall, Marshall H. *Human Behavior in Global Perspective: An Introduction to Cross-cultural Psychology*. New York: Allyn and Bacon, 1990.

Sehert, Keith W. M.D. *Stress/Unstress: How You Can Control Stress at Home and on the Job*. Minneapolis: Augsburg Publishing House, 1981.

Sturgeon, Wina. *Depression: How to Recognize It and How to Grow From It*. Englewood Cliffs, NJ: Prentice-Hall, 1979.

Ting-Toomey, Stella, and Korzenny, Felipe, eds. *Cross-cultural Interpersonal Communication*. Newberry Park, CA: Sage Publications, 1991.

Triandis, C. Henry, and Lambert, William Wilson. *Handbook of Cross-cultural Psychology*. Boston: Allyn and Bacon, 1981.

Williamson, Lamar. *Ishaku: An African Christian Between Two Worlds*. Lima, O: Fairway Press, 1992.

World Vision International. *Cross-cultural Communications Bibliography*. World Vision International, 1982.

Yamamori, Tetsunao; Myers, Bryant L.; and Conner, David; eds. *Serving the Poor in Asia*. Monrovia, Calif.: MARC, 1995.

Index